The Capitol and the Campus

STATE RESPONSIBILITY
FOR POSTSECONDARY EDUCATION

A Report and Recommendations by

The Carnegie Commission on Higher Education

APRIL 1971

MCGRAW–HILL BOOK COMPANY

New York   St. Louis   San Francisco   Düsseldorf
London   Sydney   Toronto   Mexico   Panama
Johannesburg   Kuala Lumpur   Montreal
New Delhi   Rio de Janeiro   Singapore

The views and conclusions expressed in this report
are solely those of the members of the Carnegie Commission
on Higher Education and do not necessarily reflect the
views or opinions of the Carnegie Corporation of New York,
The Carnegie Foundation for the Advancement of Teaching,
or their trustees, officers, directors, or employees.

Additional copies of this report may be ordered from
McGraw-Hill Book Company, Hightstown, New Jersey 08520.
The price is $2.95 a copy.

Foreword

In December 1968, the Carnegie Commission on Higher Education issued its first Special Report, *Quality and Equality: New Levels of Federal Responsibility for Higher Education*. A supplement to that Report was issued in June 1970. That Report, concerned with the relationship between higher education and the federal government, made a series of recommendations calling for a fourfold expansion by 1976 in federal funds for higher education. This new level of federal aid, the Commission stated, is essential if our colleges and universities are to meet the nation's expectations for substantially expanding educational opportunity while protecting academic quality.

Although the crucial role of the state in helping to achieve these higher educational goals was an element in setting the new levels of federal aid, the first Report did not focus on the relationship between the state and higher education, nor did it include any Commission recommendations about that relationship.

This Report, *The Capitol and the Campus,* will examine the state's responsibility for the postsecondary education of its citizens. The Report will review and make recommendations upon state planning for postsecondary education and its coordination, upon state financing, and upon problems of public accountability and institutional independence in the context of state financial support for both public and private sectors.

In 1966, the Center for Research and Development in Higher Education and the Western Interstate Commission for Higher Education held a conference on higher education and the states. The Commission not only benefited from the several excellent papers published from that conference but chose a slight variation of the conference title, Campus and Capitol, as the title for this Report.

We wish to express our appreciation to those researchers in higher education who were kind enough to consult with the staff at various stages in the preparation of this Report: Robert Berdahl, professor, Department of Higher Education, State University of New York, Buffalo; M. M. Chambers, Department of Educational Administration, Illinois State University; Lyman Glenny, associate director, Center for Research and Development in Higher Education, University of California, Berkeley; Lewis Mayhew, professor of education, Stanford University; T. R. McConnell, professor emeritus, Department of Education, and research educator, Center for Research and Development in Higher Education, University of California, Berkeley; Ernest Palola, research specialist in sociology, Center for Research and Development in Higher Education, Berkeley. We also wish to thank the many who read and commented on preliminary drafts of the report, particularly Winfred Godwin, director, Southern Regional Education Board; Ralph Huitt, executive director, National Association of State Universities and Land-Grant Colleges; Richard Millard, director, Higher Education Services, Education Commission of the States; Fred Ness, director, Association of American Colleges; Laurence Poston, associate secretary, American Association of University Professors; Alan Ostar, director, American Association of State Colleges and Universities; and Logan Wilson, president, American Council on Education.

And finally, we wish to thank the members of our staff, and particularly Virginia B. Smith, for their work in preparing this report.

Eric Ashby
The Master
Clare College
Cambridge, England

Ralph M. Besse
Chairman of the Board
National Machinery Company

Joseph P. Cosand
President
The Junior College District
of St. Louis

William Friday
President
University of North Carolina

The Honorable Patricia
Roberts Harris
Partner
Strasser, Spiegelberg, Fried, Frank,
and Kampelman, Attorneys

David Henry
President
University of Illinois

$\mathcal{C}$ontents

The Capitol and the Campus

1. Major Themes

The major themes of this report are:

1 Among governmental units, the states have had the primary responsibility for the development of higher education throughout the history of the United States; before independence, this responsibility was carried by the colonies beginning with the support given to Harvard in 1636 by the Massachusetts Bay Colony.

2 That this responsibility generally has been well discharged is demonstrated by the quantitative and qualitative growth that has given this country a position of world leadership in higher education. The states, in the 1960s in particular, gave spectacular support to higher education in the face of a "tidal wave" of students. Their greatest previous contribution came about a century ago when the land-grant universities were being born.

3 The states should continue to carry the primary governmental responsibility for higher education they have borne historically. They have done well with it. Their guardianship has led to substantial diversity, to adaptation to regional needs, and to competitive efforts at improvement.

4 The United States should not move in the direction of a single national system of higher education as have many other nations. Our earlier recommendations for federal support emphasized its increased role—but for *specialized* purposes, such as research and student aid, and for *supplemental* purposes, such as cost-of-education allowances to institutions. We do not favor having the federal government become a dominant source of basic financial support for institutions of higher education generally, and thus potentially the dominant source of influence and control. The state-by-state system, with regional cooperation whenever appropriate, should be preserved and improved instead.

5 The states should broaden the scope of their responsibility to encompass the whole range of postsecondary education, not just the colleges and universities, and to provide universal access to post-secondary education.

6 The Commission is concerned with the growing dominance of governors over higher education in several of the states. With public attention focused on higher education and with state funding so important, governors, if they so choose, are in positions to become the most dominant forces. Sometimes this has been for the better and sometimes for the worse. But, generally, we believe that governors should not be the dominant forces in higher education. Consequently, we recommend that the appointment of members of governing boards, coordinating councils, and other such agencies be subject, as they now are in many states, to confirmation by the state senates, and not subject alone to the judgment of the governors. We also recommend that governors not serve as chairmen or members of such agencies since, as governors, they will need to review the actions of these independent agencies uncommitted by their own earlier participation as members—just as they review the actions of many other independent boards. The standard system of checks and balances, and the standard rule of avoidance of conflict of interests should apply to the relationship of governors to higher education.

7 The Commission is also concerned with the development of heavy-handed regulatory councils over higher education. Too often they add little other than another bureaucracy on top of existing bureaucracies. We see no need for duplicating the functions already performed by the states' administrative staffs, particularly the departments of finance, and the legislatures and their committees.

8 Two functions, however—long-range planning and current consultation—are not duplicative and do need to be performed by a state coordinating agency. We emphasize the great importance of effective long-range planning, of constant consultation within

higher education, and of consultation between higher education and other directly interested agencies. The new coordinating systems serve best when they concentrate on planning and consultation, rather than on routine administrative tasks, bureaucratic controls, and detailed regulation. They should provide enlightened guidance and not stifling delay and restraint. Routine regulation and control are neither needed nor compatible with the statesmanlike planning and advice that are so essential.

9 State financial support for higher education varies greatly from state to state. Generally, the Southwest and the West give greater support than the South and the Northeast, although patterns are changing. We believe that all states can and will give greater support to higher education to meet the expansion and quality needs of the 1970s. We believe, in particular, that states should make an *emergency* effort where:

a *Less than 70 percent of high school students graduate from high school. The following states failed to meet this test in 1969:*
Alabama
Georgia
Kentucky
Louisiana
Mississippi
North Carolina

b *Less than 0.6 percent of per capita income is spent through state and local taxes for higher education. The following states failed to meet this test in 1967–68:*
Connecticut
Delaware
Maine
Massachusetts
New Hampshire
New Jersey
Ohio
Pennsylvania
Virginia

c *Less than 30 places are provided by public and private higher education in the state for every 100 young people of college age. The following states failed to meet this test in 1968:*

Alaska

Georgia

Nevada

South Carolina

Virginia

d *A state's net export of students is greater than 15,000. The following states had net exports greater than this in the fall of 1968:*

Connecticut

Illinois

Maryland

New Jersey

New York

The first test determines how many young people will have a chance at postsecondary education if they want it. The second test indicates the potential quality and quantity of opportunities in higher education as made possible through public support. The third and fourth tests indicate whether a state, compared with other states, is carrying its minimum share of the burden of providing places.

10 We favor some state support of private colleges and universities. Their graduates and the graduates of public institutions benefit society equally. The private institutions also provide diversity, innovative opportunities, models of interest in the individual students, and standards of autonomy useful to all higher education. We favor state subsidy of tuition costs for students who do not have financial ability to meet these costs, leaving to the federal government the basic responsibility for subsistence costs. Tuition charges vary much more from state to state than do subsistence costs and are much more responsive to state policy. We envision tuition generally rising with per capita disposable income with a gradual narrowing of the gap between private and public tuition. We also favor state contractual support for special endeavors, such as medical schools, and greater state use of construction grants or establishment of state-created bond-issuing agencies for loans for the benefit of private as well as public institutions. When this aid is not sufficient, we favor subsidies, on a per-student basis, of up to one-third of the subsidy given students in state institutions. A full effort should be made to preserve the private sector in a condition of health and vigor.

11 Autonomy of institutions of higher education neither can be nor should be complete. The public has clear interests in their conduct. However, too often and too increasingly, autonomy is being infringed upon beyond the requirements of protecting the essential interests of the public. We suggest the limits which should be placed on external governmental interference in the internal life of the campus. As private colleges become increasingly public assisted, the establishment of such limits becomes of even greater importance. At the same time, we recognize that autonomy is to be earned by conduct, as well as claimed by right. The campus earns its autonomy as it preserves its intellectual independence from attack from within, as well as from without; as it provides high-quality instruction, research, and services; as it prevents use of its resources for electoral political purposes and commercial activities unrelated to its educational functions; as it maintains vitality and flexibility; and as it respects the democratic processes of society, as much as it demands respect for its own academic freedom.

12 As goes state support, as goes state understanding, as goes state acceptance of autonomy, so also goes, beyond any other external influence, the future of all higher education in the United States.

2. The Goal and the Issues

Throughout the history of this nation, state governments have been the public agencies most directly concerned with the education beyond high school of America's youth.

From the early chartering of private institutions of higher education to the subsequent creation of state colleges and universities and, more recently, to support of the community college movement and to overall planning and coordinating, state governments have provided initiative and funds, and have exercised some control over the postsecondary educational institutions of their states. The specific mix of funding, initiative, and control has changed over time and has varied with the particular geographic, economic, political, and cultural circumstances of the individual states, giving the United States an unusually diverse system of higher education.

Largely through state effort, higher education has ceased to be the privilege of a few and has become a possibility for the majority of high school graduates. Certain municipalities and counties also have aided this effort by establishing urban universities (University of Louisville, 1789; University of Cincinnati, 1819; City University of New York, 1847; Washburn University of Topeka, 1865; University of Akron, 1870; Municipal University of Toledo, 1872; and the Municipal University of Omaha, 1908). More recently, cities and local districts have contributed greatly to the expansion of higher education by creating hundreds of new community colleges.

THE GOAL   Regardless of the shifting nature of each state's relationships with its postsecondary educational institutions, the central goal has remained the same: to meet in one or another way the needs of its citizens for training beyond the high school. This goal has been

7

achieved with considerable success in the past. But the needs are continuing to expand and evolve:

· For training for greater proportions of the population
· For training of citizens over more of their lifetimes
· For broader ranges and alternative choices in types of training
· For higher levels of training

Beyond the individual's demands, state and societal demands on the educational system are also growing and becoming more complex:

· For expertise that will aid in solving today's social problems
· For manpower training geared to the state's changing employment patterns

To meet successfully these expanding educational needs, each state will now have to devote even greater efforts than before to the effective development and strengthening of a pluralistic system of postsecondary education.

These goals suggest that state governments should broaden the focus on higher education that prevails today. Even in a state like New York, where the scope of authority of the Board of Regents is broadly defined in legislation, the Board's activities in higher education have only recently begun to broaden beyond the chartering of institutions and registering of programs.

As it is usually defined, higher education encompasses only public and private two-year and four-year colleges and universities. Defined in this way, higher education includes some 2,500 institutions and about 8 million students. *Postsecondary education* more broadly defined, however, also includes private profit and non-profit trade and technical schools, public adult and area vocational schools, and various trade union apprenticeship programs as essential elements in state educational planning. Under this definition, postsecondary education includes not only the 2,500 colleges and universities but also approximately 7,000 private trade and technical schools, and at least 500 apprenticeship programs, adult public schools, and correspondence schools bringing the number of institutions to about 10,000 and bringing the total enrollment to about 10 million.

Unfortunately, data that can be used for comparative purposes is limited mainly to information about colleges and universities. Thus our present capacity to examine fully the state's relationships to the totality of postsecondary education is restricted by past failures to view it as a totality and by tendencies to omit private institutions from state concern.

CRITERIA OF SUCCESS The Carnegie Commission believes that the following are appropriate criteria by which a state government can evaluate its progress in meeting the goal of a strong and effective system of postsecondary education for all its citizens:

- The system offers universal access to postsecondary education related to the needs and qualifications of each student.

- It assures economic equality of educational opportunity.

- It assures that instruction will be high quality at all levels and for all academic or vocational fields.

- It encourages diversity, avoids moving toward homogeneity, and fosters a broad range of academic, technical, professional, and vocational options.

- It preserves fundamental institutional autonomy and integrity while recognizing the need for appropriate kinds of public accountability.

- It continues, to the extent possible, the present pattern of diversification of funding in order to enhance both the diversity of the system and the autonomy of the individual institutions.

- It helps to preserve a strong segment of private postsecondary education.

- It responds effectively to manpower needs.

- It provides incentives for desirable innovation.

- It supplies adequate state assistance to meet these needs.

THE ISSUES The evolving nature of the relationships between campus and capitol has brought to the forefront some crucial issues that bear directly on the ability of state governments to meet their goals for postsecondary education in the decade of the seventies. Among the questions this report will examine and seek to answer are these:

1 Should state governments continue to have primary responsibility for planning and developing a postsecondary education system?

2 Do the present levels and potentials for increase in state financial support appear to be adequate to achieve the postsecondary educational goals?

3 What are the effects of the more rapid rise in tuition at private rather than at public institutions?

4 Should more states grant public funds to private colleges and universities?

5 What are the reasonable limits to the degree of institutional control that should accompany grants of public funds?

6 How can states plan most effectively for a maximum state postsecondary education effort?

3. Nature of State Responsibility

In 1967–68, approximately two-thirds of the nation's college and university income from public sources came from state and local governments. If the proposals for increased federal aid made by the Carnegie Commission in its first report, *Quality and Equality,* were implemented, the state and local proportions of the public contribution would drop, although the absolute amounts would have to be increased. Should this potential change in the relative financial roles of state and federal governments carry with it an implied change in locus of major responsibility for expanding and strengthening a pluralistic system of postsecondary education? Beyond the question of funding, do the growing concerns for a nationally integrated system of postsecondary education providing substantially equal opportunities regardless of state of residence demand that the exercise of state responsibility be subordinated to that of the nation? Or should both state and federal responsibility be curtailed and greater reliance be placed on the marketplace as regulator? Answers to these questions depend in part on the special nature of state governments' responsibility for postsecondary education, a responsibility that has been shaped by the nature of our federal structure, the existence of a private sector, and the development of local institutions.

THE FEDERAL STRUCTURE   Unlike the governments of most other nations, the federal government of the United States has had a limited role in planning, developing, and funding education. Since power over education is not specifically granted to the federal government in the Constitution, it has been assumed that this power is reserved to the states. The federal government is not precluded, however, from expressing interest, giving encouragement, and providing financial aid. As early as 1785 and again in 1787, federal laws set aside public lands for endowment of schools. The Ordinance of 1787 declared, "religion, morality, and knowledge being necessary to good government and the happiness of mankind, schools and the means of education shall forever be encouraged." Through financial support, the federal government has influenced development of certain educational programs throughout the range of American education and, particularly at the higher education level, has encouraged development of certain types of institutions. Since World War II, the federal government has become more deeply involved in education through substantial funding of university-based research, financial aid programs for college and university students, and enforcement of constitutional rights.

The role of the federal government as educational entrepreneur, however, has been limited almost completely to military service education and to establishment of schools in the District of Columbia. The federal government has restricted its higher education responsibility to satisfaction of special national needs such as scientific research or increasing equal opportunity, and has left to the states the major responsibility for the totality of their educational programs.

PRIVATE INSTITUTIONS While it is the state rather than the federal government that has major responsibility for postsecondary education, the nature of that responsibility is affected in every state by the existence of private educational institutions. The proportion of college and university enrollment in private institutions varies greatly from state to state (see Map 1 and Appendix A).

The states, and earlier the colonies, originally relied on private initiative to found and control institutions which would serve the educational needs of the community. Early American legislatures not only granted charters to corporate or other governing bodies to found educational institutions—making them and not the state responsible for internal control—but the legislatures also came to their aid with grants of funds (for example, Harvard, Yale, Bowdoin, Williams, Columbia), land-grants (for example, Dartmouth), and state-authorized lotteries (for example, Princeton, Union, Williams). Legislatures gave these institutions tax-exempt status and exempted members of collegiate communities from taxation and militia duty. In turn, the colleges fulfilled their public responsibilities by providing the type of educational services which society seemed to need.

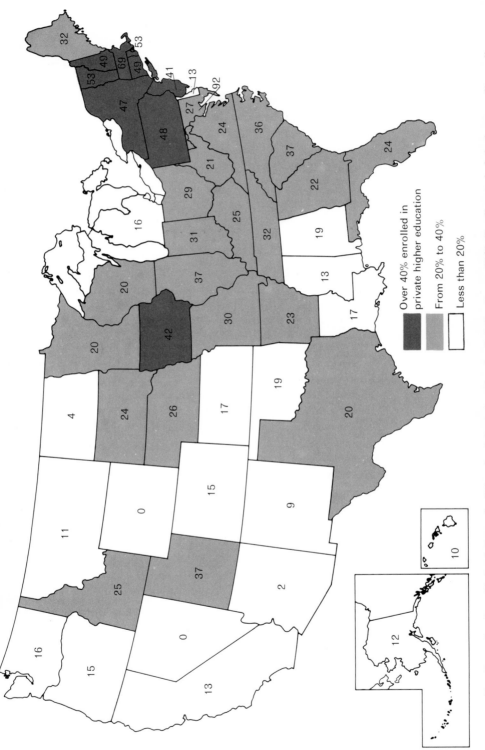

SOURCE: Enrollment data from National Center for Educational Statistics, *Opening Fall Enrollment*, 1968. Enrollments include degree-credit enrollment (both extension and resident) at all institutions listed in the U. S. Office of Education Directory of Institutions of Higher Education.

Over 40% enrolled in private higher education

From 20% to 40%

Less than 20%

For well over a century of American higher education, from the founding of Harvard in 1636 to the founding of the first public institution, the University of Georgia in 1785, public colleges and universities did not exist. By 1800, North Carolina, Tennessee, and Vermont had established state institutions. At the beginning of the nineteenth century, the states began to take more interest in the management of the private institutions. There were brief take-overs of institutions by state governments and movements to include state officials on governing boards. The efforts to establish various degrees of public control over private institutions were rebuffed in several court decisions culminating in the Dartmouth College case in 1819.

The decision in the Dartmouth case denied the governor and the legislature any right to control the college. Basing his decision on the constitutional prohibition that states may not impair the obligation of contracts, Chief Justice Marshall in his opinion for the Court stated that:

The founders of the college contracted, not merely for the perpetual application of the funds which they gave, to the objects for which those funds were given; they contracted also, to secure that application by the constitution of the corporation. They contracted for a system, which should, as far as human foresight can provide, retain forever the government of the literary institution they had formed, in the hands of persons approved by themselves. This system is totally changed. The charter of 1769 exists no longer. It is reorganized; and reorganized in such a manner, as to convert a literary institution, moulded according to the will of its founders, and placed under the control of private literary men, into a machine entirely subservient to the will of government. This may be for the advantage of this college in particular, and may be for the advantage of literature in general; but it is not according to the will of the donors, and is subversive of that contract, on the faith of which their property was given. . . .[1]

This decision protected what increasingly would be known as *private colleges* from legislative control and gave great encouragement to the establishment of *church colleges* as well as independent private colleges. With this encouragement, private colleges continued to dominate higher education until the Civil War and the passage of the Morrill federal land grant act of 1862.

---

[1] *Dartmouth College v. Woodward,* 4 Wheat. 518, 4 L.Ed. 629 (1819), p. 525.

By 1900, 47 states had established state colleges and universities; states had gained importance as educational entrepreneurs. In 1900, enrollment in private institutions had dropped to 62 percent of all college and university students, and by 1920 the figure had fallen to 47 percent. The proportion of private enrollment declined only slightly from 1920 to 1960, when it reached 43 percent, but fell sharply in the next eight years to 28 percent in 1969 (see Figure 1). If enrollment in two-year colleges is excluded, however, private enrollment constitutes a third, rather than a little over a fourth, of total enrollment.

LOCAL PUBLIC INSTITUTIONS   Enrollment in public two-year colleges increased fivefold in the 1960s. These institutions were often established, controlled, and partially financed by local governments. In those states in which community colleges are the result of local initiative and rely heavily on local support, state responsibility for postsecondary education has been significantly modified. Massive expansion of locally controlled two-year institutions has caused problems of articulation between the community colleges and other state institutions, of

FIGURE 1   *Percent of university and college students enrolled in private institutions, 1636–1785 and 1899–1969 (includes enrollment at two-year institutions)*

SOURCE: Comparable data is not available for the period prior to 1899, but it is well documented that the first public institution in the present sense of the term was established in 1785. Source for the years 1899 to 1969 is the *Digest of Educational Statistics,* 1969, table 3, and *Opening Fall Enrollment,* U.S. Office of Education, Washington, D.C., 1969.

shifts in patterns of public support, and of expanded needs for student financial aid for transfer students.

As the community college movement expands, local governments are finding it difficult to obtain the necessary financial resources to support the colleges. Many community colleges are calling for greater state support. This issue was discussed in an earlier Commission report, *The Open-Door Colleges,* which makes recommendations concerning the state relationship to community colleges.

The federal structure and the role of private and locally supported institutions, combined with the particular geographic settings and the social, political, and economic patterns of the different states, lead the Carnegie Commission to believe that the state governments are the units in our society best situated to exercise the major responsibility for postsecondary education. Even if our federal structure permits a national system, such a system would probably be undesirable because of its likely inability to respond sufficiently to the different patterns of postsecondary education already existing in the various states or to the states varying cultural and economic needs. Local governments, on the other hand, are too limited in terms of resources and represent too narrow a community to supply an adequate range of postsecondary options.

The Carnegie Commission recommends that state governments continue to exercise major responsibility, in cooperation with local governments and private institutions, for maintaining, improving, and expanding systems of postsecondary education adequate to meet the needs of the American people.

The Commission has recommended in its report *Quality and Equality* that the federal government should continue to provide urgently needed aid for special purposes, including limited institutional assistance to the nation's colleges and universities, and a program of student grants and loans to increase access to postsecondary education. The Commission assumed in that report that private sources would continue to account for about half of total higher education income.

In its report *The Open-Door Colleges,* the Commission recommended continuation of local involvement in establishing, funding, and controlling community colleges. In technical and vocational education, local governments and private agencies presently play and will undoubtedly continue to play important roles.

But the continuing state responsibility, as recommended above, is both residual and pivotal. The state need not and should not directly supply all the resources necessary, nor should it exercise complete control over the system of postsecondary education—but it must assure that such a system exists through a multiplicity of public and private resources and institutions of various types. The state role in assuring such a system is shaped in large part by the educational policies and practices of the governor and his staff, and the legislature.

4. The Governor, the Legislature, and Higher Education

The potential influence of a governor over public higher education in his state is perhaps greater than any other single force affecting the state's public colleges and universities.

It is the governor who:

- Has final power to approve or disapprove in whole (or, in some states, item-by-item) the budget allocations from state funds to colleges and universities

- Appoints, sometimes without review or consent of any other body, the members of governing boards of public universities and colleges, and the members of state coordinating and/or planning agencies

- Serves perhaps as active chairman, more often as voting ex-officio member, of the governing boards of public institutions in many states

- As the state leader of his political party, often provides strong leadership to other ex-officio members of the board who are in his party

- Has power to sign into law or veto legislation which directly or indirectly affects higher education

- In some states, has authority to review and approve or disapprove master plans for university and college growth in the state

- Most decisively affects public attitudes toward higher education

It is evident that these formidable powers can profoundly affect, positively or negatively, higher education in the state. Recent years provide excellent examples of both impacts. Not the least impact results from the presence in some states of the governor as a voting member of an agency (the governing board) seeking public funds and, at a later stage, as the final authority over budget allocations. This double involvement may unduly influence the board's decisions on requesting funds. The standard American political system of checks and balances and the standard rule of avoidance of conflict of interest should apply to the relationship of governors to higher education.

The best assurance that a governor's various powers to appoint higher education officials will be used well is to elect a governor who understands the importance of a healthy college and university system to the growth and development of the state. It is doubtful that even the most carefully designed procedural safeguards can overcome this lack of understanding when it occurs. Nonetheless, one measure relating to the governor's power to appoint, the requirement that appointments of members of state university and college governing boards and coordinating agencies be made with the advice and consent of the state senate, does seem advisable. This requirement already exists in many states, and the Commission believes the opportunities for prior review and consultation which it affords make it a useful device for all states.

The Commission recommends:

1   That governors not serve as chairmen or voting members of state coordinating agencies or governing boards of colleges and universities; and

2   That appointments by the governor to governing boards of state colleges and universities, and to state coordinating and/or planning agencies, be made with the advice and consent of the senate.

Budget review as it relates to both the executive and legislative branches is discussed in Section 11 of this report.

Almost more important than the legal powers he possesses is the governor's ability to influence the political climate concerning higher education in the state. His willingness to make it a political issue and his treatment of that issue can have more serious consequences than any of his appointment powers. This influence is also held by members of the state legislature. While public influence is too important an aspect of the executive and legislative role not to mention, it is again the quality of those elected, rather than the particular structure within which they function, which emerges as the key element. Greater consideration is given, however, in Section 11 to the possibilities of protecting institutional independence from undue political influence.

THE LEGISLATURE   In a recently published Carnegie Commission study, *State Officials and Higher Education* by Heinz Eulau and Harold Quinley (McGraw-Hill Book Company, New York, 1970), the authors set forth the importance of state legislators in higher education, stating that they are "strategic decision makers in politics affecting higher education. The resources mobilized for colleges and universities, the goals to which such resources are allocated, and how they are distributed depend to a great extent on the views and decisions of the nation's legislative bodies."

As reported in this study, legislators:

- Have a great faith in higher education as evidenced by their tripling appropriations for it over the past decade

- Are aware that parent-constituents want educational opportunities for their children

- Have a tendency to give importance to interstate competition for a prestige system of higher education

- Strongly support those public service activities of colleges and universities designed to solve problems that affect the welfare of the state and its people

- View with favor long-range planning of higher education and centralized coordination as a means of making good use of resources and of expressing the will of the state government

- Welcome the approach of federal aid and prefer that it be spent through state governments

- Strongly support community colleges

- Are cautious toward state support for private colleges and universities

- Have a substantial degree of understanding of student dissent but clearly prefer a firm hand in dealing with it

- Give low priority to expenditures on university research

- Feel remote from the complex operations, including finances, of the university

Apart from its budget appropriation functions, perhaps the single most significant power of the state legislature over the state's colleges and universities is in coordination. While the planning functions may be carried on in another agency, in many states the ultimate authority for plan approval rests with the legislature, and in all states significant elements of the plans cannot be implemented without legislative appropriations. It is the legislature that creates the structure for coordination in the state and it is the legislature that, in most instances, provides the impetus and mechanisms for planning. The nature of the mechanisms established and the delineation of authority and responsibilities delegated by the legislature to coordinating and planning agencies, play key roles in the development of the state system.

5. Coordination and Planning

At the beginning of the twentieth century, most of America's 1,000 public and private colleges and universities operated as separate entities, a pattern that had persisted for more than two centuries. But operation as separate institutions, particularly for publicly supported colleges and universities, became both less feasible and less desirable in the twentieth century. Developing pressures demanded the creation of new relationships among the units and a revision of patterns for interaction with the state government.

- By 1960 the number of institutions had doubled, bringing the total number of colleges and universities to over 2,000.

- In 1900 educational and general income of institutions was approximately $40 million. By 1960 this amount was more than 100 times as great, and in 1969 educational and general income of colleges and universities was more than 300 times as great as it was at the turn of the century.

- Within the first three decades of the twentieth century, enrollment in higher education quadrupled; in the second three decades it tripled; and in the past decade alone it doubled. Ninety-seven percent of the expansion in total higher education enrollment since 1636 occurred in the twentieth century.

- By 1900 the era of public higher education was well under way, and demands on state funds began to grow rapidly. Between 1910 and 1964 state expenditures on higher education increased one hundredfold, from $21 million to $2.1 billion.

- In 1900 federal funds for higher education were minimal, but by the 1960s federal programs made substantial funds available to colleges and universities, and state agencies had to be developed under some of these programs to channel funds to institutions.

This growth in size and complexity inevitably led to some undesirable competition and duplication. And the increased public commitment to equality of educational opportunity and universal access to higher education portended even greater pressures in the decades ahead.

The relationship which emerged in response to these pressures resulted for the most part from state initiative and took the form of consolidating several units under a single governing board or establishing coordinating agencies. In addition, states have increasingly favored various types of overall educational planning.

FORMS OF STATE COOR-DINATION

The term *coordination* implies the existence of separate units, each with some freedom to control its own operations, and thus the need for a technique or mechanism by which they can act together toward some purpose that cannot be achieved by isolated, individual actions.

In such a mechanism, the requisites for success are the ability of the coordinating agency to be persuasive and the willingness of the units to subordinate their individual interests to common goals.

Governing boards, often considered a form of coordination although not strictly within the definition, generally have more power than coordinating agencies and thus need not rely to the same extent on persuasion. While an effective governing agency must be responsive to the individual interests of its units, to the extent that it controls budget and personnel selection, it usually has the added dimension of helping to shape those interests.

Mechanisms employed by the state range along this entire continuum of voluntary coordination among sovereign units to subordination of all units to a single governing board. Prior to 1940, 15 states placed all public institutions under single governing boards. In a sense, these states eliminated the need for coordination by creating one governmental unit.

In the next two decades, 12 states adopted some form of coordinating agency rather than establishing single governing boards. This suggested a trend away from centralization of authority and toward a separation of coordinating functions from governing functions. This trend may, however, be short-lived. In the last few years, three additional states have brought all their public institutions under single governing boards, and other states are seriously considering this approach. (See Appendix B for summary of state coordination agencies.)

A single governing board is unlikely to be the most appropriate form of coordination except for small states with relatively little private higher education, very few public institutions, and generally a simple postsecondary system. Even in such a state, the desire to include the state's vocational institutions, community colleges, and private colleges and universities in the coordinating process may lead to the need for a coordinating agency. It is possible that some of the states are well served by single governing boards because of a particular combination of history and present circumstances. Such states may, however, find it absolutely essential to create separate planning agencies, since the single governing board with its great concern for administrative functions, is usually not well suited for planning functions.

At the other end of the continuum is voluntary coordination through agencies which are without regulatory powers established by the institutions themselves. This form, which was urged by leading educators in mid-century as the most desirable type of coordination for higher education, did not prove entirely effective. Perhaps there was insufficient acceptance of common goals and too great an adherence to the aims of individual institutions. Today, voluntary coordination is used by only one state. It is, however, becoming increasingly important for private institutions which have realized that efforts to obtain public funding or increased private funds might better be accomplished on a coordinated basis. Voluntary coordination efforts, including consortia, seem most appropriate in those situations where there is:

1   A quite visible community of interest (such as a mutually advantageous desire to share specified facilities or programs)

2   A necessity for including units responsible to jurisdictions of different states (such as the need to mobilize educational resources of urban areas involving more than one state to meet the special educational needs of that area, or the desire to establish information systems which include some degree of comparability among the data of various states)

Coordinating boards created by law, as contrasted with those created voluntarily by the constituents, now exist in 27 states. These agencies have specifically defined responsibilities, some with certain delegated authorities and some with advisory functions only. Typically the coordinating agency does not control adminis-

States with:	1939*	1949*	1959	1964	1969
No formal coordination	33	28	17	11	3
Voluntary coordination	0	3	7	4	1
Coordination boards	2	3	10	18	27
Advisory	(1)	(1)	(5)	(11)	(13)
Regulatory	(1)	(2)	(5)	(7)	(14)
Consolidated governing board	15	16	16	17	19

*Including the territories of Alaska and Hawaii.

SOURCE: Adapted from a study on state coordination by Robert Berdahl to be published soon by the American Council on Education.

trative detail such as hiring and firing of institutional personnel or control budget at the operational levels. The particular mix of advisory and regulatory responsibilities varies from state to state. The boards in 13 states might be characterized as primarily advisory, while the remaining 14 are more regulatory in nature.

The above table shows the change in form and nature of state coordinating agencies over the last three decades.

PURPOSES OF COORDINATION

Regardless of the form the coordinating agencies take, they are usually established to achieve the following:

- Avoid wasteful duplication in programs and harmful competition for resources

- Work toward greater efficiency in the use of scarce resources

- Aid the orderly growth of all postsecondary facilities within the state, including consideration of locations for new campuses

- Assist in developing state policy on admission of students to higher education

- Collect data needed for policy determination

- Encourage sufficient diversity within the system to satisfy the diverse educational needs of the state

- Serve as a communications agency among the postsecondary education community, the state government, and the public

- Foster excellence in the development of the variety of programs involved in the expanding postsecondary education network

Some states have been relatively successful in preventing duplication in the establishment of new programs, but relatively little success has been experienced in the elimination of existing duplication. Coordinating agencies have not exhibited much capacity for increasing diversity and have given little but lip service to fostering excellence in the educational programs of the state. On the other hand, many agencies have performed well as communicators among postsecondary education, the legislatures, and the public. However, this communication has been confined primarily to the needs for resources for expansion of the network. Although most programs for more effective use of resources have been limited to space utilization studies, achieving optimum student-teacher ratios, and year-round utilization, some have dealt with more fundamental matters of structure and function in higher education. Both the Illinois and Florida agencies have been instrumental in establishing senior colleges—certainly a structural innovation in this decade. Agencies have also experienced some success in curbing unwise expansion, in locating new campuses in urban areas, and in developing technical programs for community colleges.

Not only the competence of the staff but also the nature of the agency's authority may affect its ability to carry out this entire range of functions. Coordinating agencies with administrative responsibilities and single governing boards undoubtedly find it easier to avoid wasteful duplication than do advisory agencies. The stronger types of agencies could achieve greater efficiency in the use of scarce resources, but unduly rigid and detailed budget review approaches could actually inhibit the type of organizational innovation needed for more efficient use of resources. It is also possible that their regulatory functions could impede improvement of communications and thus affect the spirit and thoroughness with which institutions supply data. Institutions are more likely to share information in the interest of policy development or to facilitate self-study than they are to share information for the purpose of being regulated. Diversity and excellence, conceivably, could be difficult if not impossible to achieve through any but the most unusual single state governing board or highly regulatory state agency.

**COORDINAT-
ING AGENCIES
AND MULTI-
CAMPUS IN-
STITUTIONS**
A more intricate relationship than those described above is that which develops between a state coordinating agency and the board of trustees of a multicampus institution. Substantial friction between these two bodies may result when the coordinating agency is invested with administrative or detailed regulatory powers. A Carnegie Commission study under the direction of Eugene Lee will discuss the special problems of the multicampus institutions.

The Commission believes that creation of single governing boards or establishment of coordinating agencies with administrative responsibilities results in centralized detailed control leading ultimately to rigidity and conformity. Also, unnecessary layering of authority means that similar processes are carried out at successive layers, and each decision affecting the operation of an institution takes longer and is more remote from the functioning level.

The Commission further believes that coordination efforts should, to the greatest extent possible, include private as well as public institutions. Single boards or regulatory agencies are somewhat handicapped from incorporating private institutions in their activities since they have a substantially different relationship to the public institutions within their jurisdiction.

State finance or budget officers usually review budgets for higher education. Some state finance offices are not properly equipped to carry out this function, but in those states where it is performed by an existing state agency, prior budget review by the coordinating agency will not prevent the further review by the finance office. The Commission believes that budget review, whether performed by the finance office or a coordinating agency, should not be used as an indirect technique for controlling educational programs. The determination of appropriate educational programs should not be an ad hoc process occurring annually at the time of budget review, but should instead be an integral part of the educational planning for the state. Thus coordinating agencies in their roles as implementers of educational plans should be involved in the budget review process only as advisors and consultants on educational programs.

State coordinating agencies are often at a disadvantage in encouraging the development of programs designed to improve quality through experimentation and innovation. If state agencies had moderate budgets available for this purpose, they would be much more able to have a positive influence on academic quality. Funds allocated to agencies for this purpose must be in addition to basic institutional budgets in order to avoid making the agency a competitor for funds that would otherwise be channeled directly to institutions.

While recognizing the need for more effective coordination of postsecondary education at the state level, the Commission recommends that states strongly resist:

1 Investing coordinating agencies with administrative authority, particularly over budget matters, or

2   Establishing single governing boards, except in those states in which a special combination of historical factors and present circumstances make such agencies more feasible than other types of coordinating agencies.

The Commission further recommends that:

1   If an existing state agency such as the budget office or finance office undertakes budget review for higher education, the coordinating agency should not be given the responsibility for an independent budget review, but should instead be involved in the budget review process of the other state agency. This involvement should include, at the very minimum, the availability of the budget analyst's data, including the institutions' presentations and the budget department's analysis, and representatives of the coordinating agencies should attend and participate in all hearings on the appropriation request. In some instances, it may also be possible for members of the coordinating agency staff to work with the budget analyst's staff in a consultative capacity in making the budget review.

2   If there is no existing state agency which does or can undertake budget review for higher education, budget review, as opposed to budget control, could be assigned to the coordinating agency.

3   Although the Commission recommends against investing coordinating agencies with authority to control institutional budgets, it does recommend that states grant to coordinating agencies some funds which the agency itself can grant to institutions to encourage quality improvement, and experimentation and innovation consistent with the state's long-range educational goals. Agencies allocating funds for these purposes should regularly evaluate the programs developed with such funds.

4   Coordinating agencies should be assigned certain program review responsibilities and authority consistent with their educational planning functions. (The planning functions of the coordinating agency will be discussed in the next section.)

5   Coordinating agencies should act in an advisory capacity on matters such as:

· Effective use of resources

· Educational quality

· Access to postsecondary education

· Appropriate functions for the various types of institutions

- Articulation among the various elements within postsecondary education

6 Coordinating agencies should serve as a buffer and communicator

- Explaining the above matters to agencies of the state government and to the public
- Developing mutual understanding of common goals among the elements of postsecondary education
- Protecting the institutions, when necessary, from legislative, executive, or public interference in carrying out their educational functions

It is often proposed that coordinating agencies be granted more authority in order to improve their performance. But the quality of performance may not be as clearly related to the authorities which they possess as to the nature of their staffs and the levels at which they are funded. Indeed, in some instances the quality of the staff is used as an argument against the assignment of further responsibilities. Many boards have been inadequately staffed, underfinanced, and have lacked in support from both public and private institutions. They have often operated within a scope too narrow to permit effective coordination of the totality of postsecondary education and have functioned in the absence of well-defined goals and purposes to guide their coordination efforts.

The Commission recommends:

That states review the funding levels of their coordinating agencies to determine if the levels permit attention to the broader functions of coordination or only to those minimal duties legally required of the agencies.

That states take steps to attract staff members of the ability, stature, and sensitivity required to carry out the complex tasks of the agencies (e.g., salary level increases, opportunities for educational and research leaves, and adoption of certain other fringe benefits usually available to members of the academic community).

That states with heavy institutional representation in the composition of their boards take steps to increase the proportion of lay members and to introduce appropriate nominating techniques for appointment of outstanding noninstitutional members, regardless of who has the final appointing authority.

That boards seek to increase acceptance by the institutions through

1   more effective consultation with the entire range of post-secondary institutions

2   experimentation with a program of limited term exchanges of personnel between agency and institutional staffs

3   establishment of joint board staff and institutional staff seminars or workshops focused on state educational concerns

That institutions examine their own levels of cooperativeness to determine whether failures to respond to advisory agencies might lead more surely and quickly to establishment of regulatory agencies.

Even if all of these recommendations were implemented, it is doubtful that a coordinating agency could function effectively in the absence of a state plan which includes both immediate and long-range goals for the system it is to coordinate.

STATEWIDE PLANNING   The basic impetus for coordination of educational units was the desire to avoid multiple budget negotiations between several separate institutions and the state legislature and to avoid competition that might be harmful to the system as a whole and to the units within it.

Planning, on the other hand, grew out of broader and more long-range concerns. In its broadest sense, statewide planning must first be concerned with sets of goals: the economic and social goals of the state, the goals of the educational system and its institutions, the goals of the individuals within the system, and the interaction among these sets of goals. Then planning must be addressed to the optimum allocation of resources to accomplish the desired ends.

Unprecedented growth during the 1950s and 1960s and anticipated continued growth in the 1970s have led many states to initiate various forms of statewide planning activities. Only 21 states, however, have undertaken comprehensive studies of needs and resources for higher education that have led to the development of formal plans.

Scope and Success of Planning   State planning activities, when supported by effective implementation of the plans by coordinating councils, governing boards, legislatures, or other agencies, have been successful in a number of significant ways:

- They have deepened the knowledge and understanding of state systems of higher education.

- They have justified to the legislature and to the public the need for increases in budgets for higher education and the institutional differences in budgetary requirements.

- They have stimulated institutions to engage in more sophisticated planning at the institutional level.

- They have facilitated orderly expansion of new campuses and new programs.

- They have led to some degree of differentiation in function among public segments (although there has been little success in achieving differentiation among institutions within segments).

In view of their relatively recent development and their initiation during a period of very rapid growth, state planning agencies can be proud of their accomplishments. It is true, however, that such agencies, whether independent from or functioning as a part of a coordinating council, are often too limited in scope and thus unable to take up crucial issues in postsecondary education.

Most state plans include some statement of goals, but these are often set forth in very broad terms and frequently without reference to the state's manpower needs or to an individual's educational needs over his lifetime as opposed to his immediate need upon completing high school. Projections of enrollments and of resource needs based on present trends are quite sophisticated in recent planning documents. Few of the projections, however, encompass the whole of postsecondary education, most being limited to colleges and universities and often only those under public control.

Relatively few state plans have explored the possible impacts of increases in tuition levels or have thoroughly analyzed the implications of interstate patterns of student migration. Few state plans have given attention to articulation with high schools. Concern with quantitative analysis seems to have overshadowed adequate interest in questions of quality, diversity, and flexibility.

What should be the content of statewide planning? The exact nature of the content and the emphasis placed on various aspects of that content will depend upon the particular circumstances in each state. The following checklist of matters that should be considered for possible inclusion in any state plan suggests the range of content.

A checklist of planning considerations

☐ Statement of goals:
  - Educational
  - Social
  - Economic
  - Individual

☐ Quantification of the goals, to the extent possible

☐ Analysis in terms of enrollment, resources, and programs of present post-secondary education in the state, including:
  - Public and private colleges and universities
  - Public and private trade and technical schools
  - Present extent of use of new educational technologies
  - Opportunities for adult training and education
  - Geographic availability of institutions in the state

☐ Projections for at least the short run (2 to 5 years) and the intermediate period (5 to 15 years), including:
  - Enrollment trends categorized by institutional type and broadly defined programs
  - State manpower needs
  - Resource requirements—including faculty (area and level), physical facilities and equipment, libraries, and funding levels for operating and capital expenses

☐ Consideration of present and potential arrangements with other states to maximize use of state resources

☐ Extent of differentiation of function among types of institutions, and plans for bringing about desired changes in the pattern of differentiation

☐ Analysis of the quality of existing programs and proposals for improvement

☐ Analysis of the present degree of efficiency in use of educational resources and proposals for increasing efficiency

☐ Definition of the state relation to private education, including descriptions of present and projected state aid to private education, if any

☐ Analysis of existing requirements for admission and recommendations for any modifications if deemed advisable

☐ Review of tuition levels at public institutions and, if any increases are projected, an analysis of the impacts of increased tuition on student financial aid requirements and enrollment at various types of institutions

☐ Attention to the articulation of postsecondary education with secondary education, including consideration of advanced placement

☐ Concern with the potential adaptability to changing educational needs of the system and the units within it

☐ Evaluation of the adequacy of counseling for careers and for postsecondary education sufficiently early in a student's life to be effective and proposals for improving the programs if necessary

☐ Identification of any other agencies outside postsecondary education which have major impacts on the way postsecondary education is able to function and suggestions for improving the interaction with these agencies

Recommen- As minimum elements in any state planning effort, the Commission
dations recommends attention be given to:

- Present and future access to postsecondary education, including need for student spaces, student financial aid programs, geographic availability of institutions, and admission standards for types of institutions

- Appropriate functions for the various types of institutions within postsecondary education, including degrees to be granted, research activities, and public service functions

- Orderly growth of postsecondary education — including location of new campuses, development of new schools, and optimum size of institutions

- Articulation among the various elements of postsecondary education and within secondary education

In setting the parameters for these planning functions, the Commission recommends that state agencies:

- Take into account the present and potential contributions to state needs of all types of postsecondary institutions including universities, colleges, private trade and technical schools, area vocational schools, industry, and unions and other agencies providing various forms of postsecondary education

- Encompass the entire timespan of a person's postsecondary education needs from immediately after high school throughout life

The Commission further recommends that states, in developing both their short- and longer-range plans, give greater attention to institutional diversity, and to building sufficient flexibility into both institutional and system-wide plans to permit adaptation as educational processes and needs change.

Responsibility for Planning There is substantial variation among the states in the type of agency assigned responsibility for planning. In some states, development of plans has been undertaken by special task forces reporting directly to the legislature. In others the planning responsibility has been assigned to the coordinating council or to the governing board, or to one or more task forces working through the governing board or council. In a few states, planning is primarily viewed as a fiscal function and is therefore delegated to the finance or budget division.

The Commission believes that a state agency with ongoing administrative duties which involve a substantial exercise of control, such as governing boards, regulatory coordinating councils, or budget offices, are not in the best position to conduct comprehensive state studies and develop statewide plans. The immediate demands of their administrative duties combined with the continuing day-to-day relations with institutions could militate against such agencies' having either the requisite time or the perspective to undertake these tasks properly. Furthermore, it is conceivable that meeting the goals of the state might require modifications in the governing board, or in a regulatory coordinating council. It is likely that such desired modifications in the central agency with authority would be seen more readily by a group other than the agency itself.

The Commission's proposed advisory functions for a coordinating agency would, on the other hand, be quite consistent with planning functions. If the scope of the coordinating agency has been broadened sufficiently to encompass the entire range of postsecondary education, and if its functions are advisory, it would be appropriate to assign at least the short-range planning function to a special staff within the coordinating agency and to assign it responsibility for implementation of plans. If these conditions are not present, it would be most desirable to assign planning functions to a continuing commission. In either case, the Commission believes, the planning staff should be kept relatively small drawing on the services of special task forces for particular aspects of reports and planning activities. Planning agencies, and the task forces working with them, should assure broad participation in the planning process by the leaders of the concerned educational constituencies, as well as including substantial public representation. The members of the planning agencies or special commission should be drawn from the most respected and experienced citizens of the state. This is the most important criterion for statewide planning.

The Commission recommends that a state's initial development of a broad postsecondary educational plan be undertaken by a commission appointed for that purpose with a small staff augmented by special task forces as needed, selected so as to assure participation by both public representatives and leaders of educational constituencies.

Periodic Review of Plans

A plan once developed is in danger of being considered more or less final and unchangeable. Planning is most valid in the short run. Intermediate and long-range planning raises questions about the continuing validity of the assumptions on which the planning is based. It is imperative, therefore, that the mechanisms for planning provide for frequent reviews and evaluations of progress.

Responsibility for development of long-range plans and the necessary short-range modifications in such plans could appropriately be assigned to a coordinating agency if the coordinating agency has not been invested with any significant measure of administrative authority over the higher education system.

The Commission recommends that a basic reassessment of a state's postsecondary educational plan be undertaken by the advisory coordinating board, if such exists, or by a commission appointed for that purpose every five or ten years or whenever it becomes apparent that such a reassessment is essential to reflect adequately the totality and interaction of changing conditions and educational needs.

Implementation of Plans

For reasons given above, the Commission does not believe that a regulatory board or a consolidated governing board, committed to routine supervision and administration, is in any position to undertake a fresh look at long-range plans. Where such boards exist, the Commission favors an independent planning commission.

Once established, plans must be implemented and be subject to short-run modification. This implementation can be carried out by whatever coordinating mechanism exists, whether advisory or regulatory or governing. This agency will need limited authority.

The Commission recommends that coordinating agencies be granted the following authorities to be exercised within the context of the long-range plans or guidelines established for the state:

1   To approve or disapprove new institutions, branches or centers, and, where appropriate, to take active steps toward the establishment of new institutions

2   To approve all new degree programs at the doctoral level, and new master's and baccalaureate programs in general fields not previously offered, and in high-cost fields

3   To allocate funds under state-administered federal programs

Generally, the Commission believes that what is needed beyond the competence of the individual institutions and of the established state administrative and legislative bodies is effective planning, not bureaucratic regulation. Coordination should take mainly the form of high level planning and not low level regulation. Regulation either interferes with the conduct of the campus or duplicates the efforts of state authorities or both.

6. Comparisons of State Effort

The Commission believes that every state should strive to create an open access system of postsecondary education—one in which admission requirements for various segments of postsecondary education within the state are such that every young American who can benefit from further education will not be barred from doing so because of past educational disadvantages or because admission requirements are not properly related to educational function. The Commission does not favor universal attendance, but it strongly urges adoption of an open access system.

Theoretical access is not enough. Effective educational opportunity requires adequate provision of student places, through appropriate geographic distribution of institutions, and through combinations of tuition and student aid policies designed to overcome economic barriers.

Because of differences in educational systems from state to state, it is not possible to make precise comparisons of state efforts to achieve these goals. Furthermore, presently available data which are sufficiently compatible to use for state comparisons exclude information on private trade and technical schools. Nonetheless, some approximation of comparative success can be obtained from examination of

- Undergraduate enrollment of state residents as a percent of the college-age population (18 to 21)
- First-time undergraduate enrollment as a percent of that year's high school graduates

Enrollment of state residents as a percent of the college-age population

In the fall of 1968, there were 41 undergraduate students in American colleges and universities for every 100 18- to 21-year-olds in

MAP 2   Ratio of residents of state enrolled as undergraduates in any state to number of 18- to 21-year-olds in state (1968)

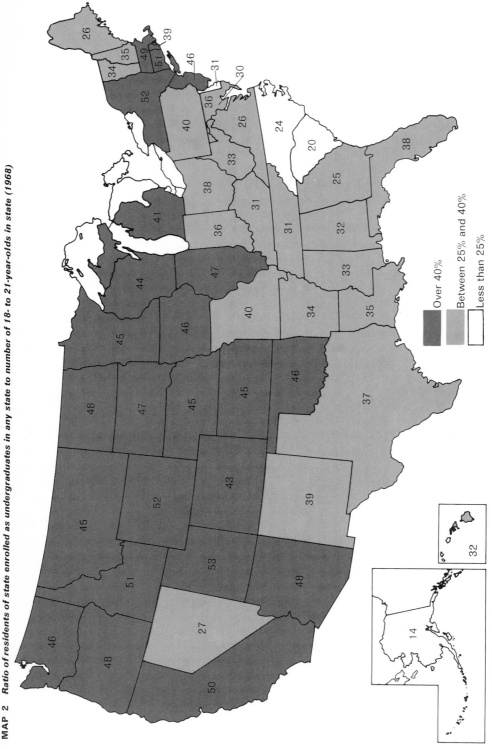

Over 40%

Between 25% and 40%

Less than 25%

32

14

SOURCE: U.S. Office of Education unpublished data on residence and migration of college students, fall 1968. Estimates derived by the Carnegie Commission staff using Bureau of the Census *Current Population Reports*, ser. P-25, nos. 375 and 416, and 1960 census data for the states.

MAP 3 Ratio of undergraduate students enrolled in state of residence to number of 18- to 21-year-olds in state (1968)

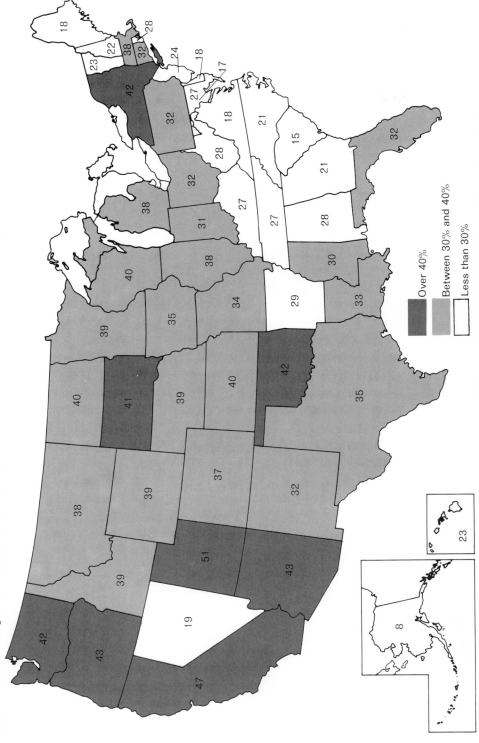

SOURCE: U.S. Office of Education unpublished data on residence and migration of college students, fall 1968. Estimates derived by the Carnegie Commission staff using Bureau of the Census *Current Population Reports*, ser. P-25, nos. 375 and 416, and 1960 census data for the states.

MAP 4 *Ratio of residents enrolled as first-time undergraduates in institutions in state to number of high school graduates (fall 1968)*

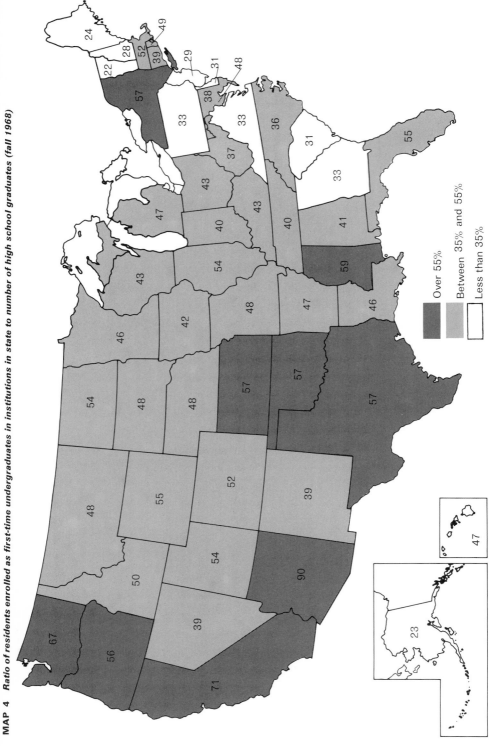

Over 55%

Between 35% and 55%

Less than 35%

SOURCE: U.S. Office of Education unpublished data on residence and migration of college students, fall 1968. U.S. Office of Education, *1969 Digest of Educational Statistics*, Washington, D.C., 1969.

MAP 5   Ratio of residents enrolled as first-time undergraduates in institutions in any state to high school graduates (1968)

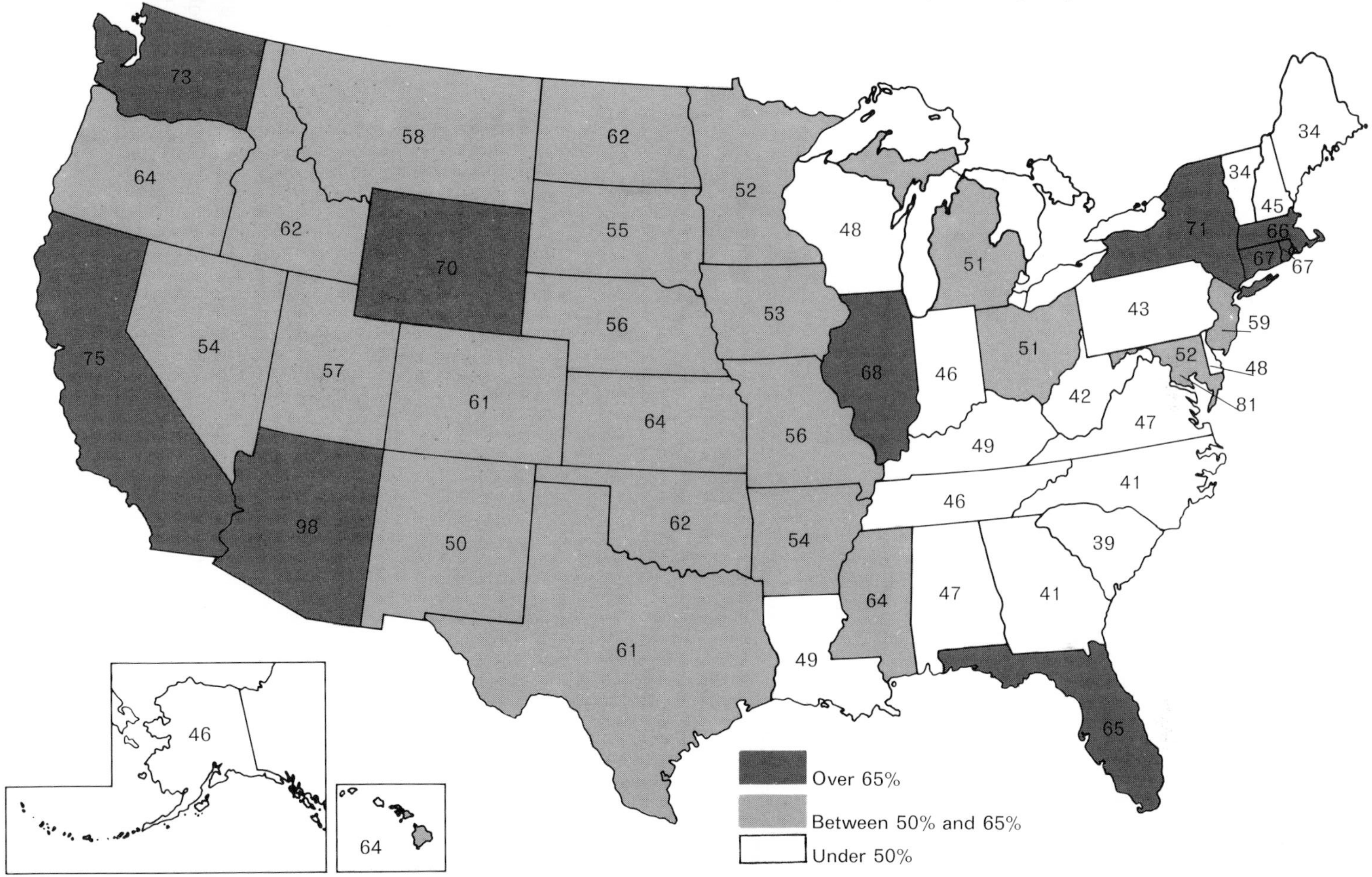

Over 65%

Between 50% and 65%

Under 50%

34

45

66   67

34   67

71

59

43   52   48   81

47   41

42   39

51   49   41   65

51   46   46   47

48   68   49

52   53   56   54   64

62   55   56   64   62   61

58   70   61   50

62   57   98

73   64   54   75

64

46

SOURCE: U.S. Office of Education unpublished data on residence and migration of college students, fall 1968. U.S. Office of Education, *1969 Digest of Educational Statistics*, Washington, D.C., 1969.

the nation. State ratios ranged from over 50 per 100 in Utah, Wyoming, California, Connecticut, Idaho, and New York to under 30 per 100 in Alaska, Maine, Nevada, South Carolina, Georgia, North Carolina, and Virginia (see Map 2 and Appendix C).

Not all students, however, enroll in institutions in their own states. On a nationwide basis, undergraduate enrollment of students remaining in their own states is 34 per 100 of 18- to 21-year-olds. State ratios range from 51 per 100 in Utah and 47 per 100 in California to less than 20 per 100 in Alaska, South Carolina, District of Columbia, Maine, Delaware, Virginia, and Nevada (see Map 3 and Appendix D).

Enrollment of first-time undergraduates as a percent of high school graduates

In the fall of 1968, 58 students enrolled for the first time in American colleges and universities for every 100 high school graduates of that year. State ratios ranged from 98 per 100 in Arizona to 34 per 100 in Vermont (see Map 4 and Appendix E).

If only those students enrolling in institutions in their own state of residence are considered, there were 48 first-time enrollees for every 100 high school graduates. State ratios ranged from 90 per 100 in Arizona to 22 per 100 in Vermont (see Map 5 and Appendix F).

In the five years between 1963 and 1968, many states greatly improved their ratios of first-time enrollment to high school graduates (see Appendix G). Arizona's ratio rose from 61 per 100 in 1963 to 98 per 100 in 1968, and New York's ratio rose from 47 per 100 to 71 per 100. The ratio in some states actually declined: California went from 81 per 100 in 1963 to 75 per 100 in 1968, and Nevada went from 70 per 100 in 1963 to 54 per 100 in 1968.[1]

REASONS FOR VARIATIONS   Of the numerous factors which undoubtedly influence the variations in state enrollment ratios described above, only three will be mentioned here. These factors, selected in large part because of their importance to state educational policy, are: (1) high school retention rates, (2) state expenditures on higher education, and (3) open access policies.

[1] Unfortunately, detailed data on migration of college students among states is available only for 1963 and 1968. Atypical conditions or circumstances in either of those years cannot be discovered by comparison with comparable data for the preceding and following years.

TABLE 2
*Public high
school
graduates in
1968–69 as
percent of
public school
ninth-graders in
fall 1965*

State	Percent
United States	78.8
Minnesota	93.4
Hawaii	91.0
Iowa	89.9
Washington	88.7
California	87.7
South Dakota	87.6
Nebraska	86.5
Pennsylvania	86.2
North Dakota	85.9
Rhode Island	85.9
Massachusetts	85.3
Utah	84.7
Wisconsin	84.6
Oregon	84.3
Idaho	84.2
Kansas	83.8
Vermont	83.5
Delaware	83.3
New Jersey	83.0
Colorado	82.9
New Hampshire	82.8
Montana	82.3
Maine	82.0
Michigan	81.7
Ohio	81.6
Connecticut	80.6
Maryland	79.2
Oklahoma	79.2
Indiana	79.1
Alaska	77.8
Illinois	77.5
New York	77.1
Wyoming	75.9
Virginia	75.6
New Mexico	75.3
Missouri	74.7

TABLE 2 *(Cont'd.)*	State	Percent
	Nevada	74.4
	West Virginia	72.9
	Arizona	72.8
	Florida	71.2
	Tennessee	71.0
	Texas	70.8
	South Carolina	70.5
	Arkansas	70.2
	Alabama	69.8
	Louisiana	69.8
	Kentucky	68.4
	Mississippi	67.6
	North Carolina	67.4
	Georgia	65.7

SOURCE: Research Division, National Education Association, *Research Report 1970-R1: Rankings of the States,* 1970, p. 28, table 48.

High School Retention Rates

As the Commission indicated in its report *A Chance to Learn,* great strides in removing barriers to equality of educational opportunity can be made only with increased attention of the state to the effectiveness of the whole range of precollege education. It is not the purpose of this report to consider the ways in which the state could improve effectiveness of the precollege educational system. It is clear, however, that in states with low high school retention rates, on the average a smaller proportion of the 18- to 21-year-olds are in college. Table 2 shows the variations in retention rates. Unfortunately the figures do not take into account interstate migration.

State Expenditures on Higher Education

There are wide variations among states in percent of per capita income spent on public higher education (see Table 3).[2] The highest rate of expenditure (Wyoming, 1.49 percent) is five times as great as the lowest state expenditure (New Jersey, 0.3 percent).

[2] There are many ways of measuring and comparing state expenditures on higher education. Each method has its own advantages and disadvantages. The method used in this section relies on data published in National Center for Educational Statistics, *Financial Statistics of Institutions of Higher Education: Current Funds, Revenues, and Expenditures, 1967–68,* and upon per capita personal income data for the same year. This method has the advantage of building into the measure state differences in population size and in levels of personal income and also utilizes data on institutional expenditures collected on a comparable basis across states. Unfortunately, the measure does not include state-financed capital expenditures and state scholarship expenditures (see

During the 14-year period from 1953–54 to 1967–68 all states significantly increased the percent of their per capita personal income spent through state and local taxes on public higher education. In 1953–54, the range was from 0.03 percent for New Jersey to 0.83 percent for North Dakota. By 1967–68, the lower limit of the range had increased to 0.3 percent for New Jersey and the high limit to 1.49 percent for Wyoming. In 1953–54, the figure for the 50 states and the District of Columbia was 0.31 percent; by 1967–68 this figure had risen to 0.74 percent.

During this period, Hawaii dramatically increased its support of higher education, rising from a rank of 32 to 6. Several other states substantially improved their rankings: Kentucky rose from 40 to 19, Arizona from 20 to 4, Alaska from 39 to 24, Wisconsin from 30 to 17, Colorado from 26 to 14, and Missouri from 45 to 34.

During the same period several Midwestern states that had ranked above the national average fell dramatically: Oklahoma fell from a rank of 4 to 36, Minnesota from 18 to 38, Kansas from 6 to 20, Iowa from 5 to 16, and Nebraska from 16 to 28.

Two Eastern states, Delaware and New Hampshire, ranked low in 1953–54, and although they doubled the percent of personal per capita income spent on higher education in the 14-year period, their ranking among the states fell even lower. Delaware fell from a position of 31 in 1953–54 to 44 in 1967–68, and New Hampshire fell from 33 to 45.

Table 7 for information on these), nor is data available for years later than 1967–68.

Another method frequently used for state comparisons is that published by M. M. Chambers and based on state appropriations for higher education (see M. M. Chambers, *Higher Education in the 50 States,* The Interstate Printers and Publishers, Inc., 1970). The Chambers approach has the advantages of utilizing current information and of including appropriations for scholarship funds. It differs from the technique used in this section in several ways. Our figures include contributions to higher education from local taxes as well as from state taxes. As community colleges, often partially supported by local taxes, become an increasingly important element in higher education, the contribution of citizens of the state to the state system through local taxes deserves consideration. There may also be differences in appropriations and actual institutional expenditures. The reader interested in comparing rankings derived from these two techniques is directed to Appendix H, where states are ranked on the basis of per capita state appropriations for higher education. Note that this reflects state differences in population but not state differences in personal income levels. Since the Commission is recommending greater contributions by states falling below certain levels, we feel it important in our measure to reflect differences in state levels of personal income as well as differences in appropriation level.

TABLE 3 *Percent of per capita income spent* on public higher education, 1953–54 to 1967–68*

State	1953–54	1967–68	Rank 1953–54	Rank 1967–68	Change in rank
Alabama	.363%	.765%	24	25	− 1
Alaska	.222	.794	39	24	+15
Arizona	.406	1.219	20	4	+16
Arkansas	.446	.833	17	21	− 4
California	.442	1.091	19	12	+ 7
Colorado	.354	1.053	26	14	+12
Connecticut	.176	.446	43	47	− 4
Delaware	.289	.535	31	44	−13
Florida	.390	.756	21	29	− 8
Georgia	.217	.726	41	35	+ 6
Hawaii	.286	1.134	32	6	+26
Idaho	.538	1.051	10	15	− 5
Illinois	.257	.745	37	31	+ 6
Indiana	.325	.825	28	23	+ 5
Iowa	.572	.994	5	16	−11
Kansas	.559	.925	6	20	−14
Kentucky	.219	.952	40	19	+21
Louisiana	.550	1.100	8	9	− 1
Maine	.184	.589	42	42	0
Maryland	.261	.613	36	41	− 5
Massachusetts	.080	.385	49	49	0
Michigan	.362	.827	25	22	+ 3
Minnesota	.445	.666	18	38	−20
Mississippi	.524	.969	11	18	− 7
Missouri	.172	.733	45	34	+11
Montana	.485	1.067	15	13	+ 2
Nebraska	.481	.758	16	28	−12
Nevada	.276	.754	34	30	+ 4
New Hampshire	.284	.498	33	45	−12
New Jersey	.033	.301	50	50	0
New Mexico	.543	1.186	9	5	+ 4
New York	.166	.618	46	40	+ 6
North Carolina	.377	.743	23	33	−10
North Dakota	.827	1.246	1	3	− 2
Ohio	.173	.432	44	48	− 4
Oklahoma	.588	.726	4	36	−32

State	1953–54	1967–68	Rank 1953–54	Rank 1967–68	Change in rank
Oregon	.507	1.128	12	7	+ 5
Pennsylvania	.084	.448	48	46	+ 2
Rhode Island	.150	.665	47	39	+ 8
South Carolina	.378	.771	22	25	− 3
South Dakota	.553	1.297	7	2	+ 5
Tennessee	.265	.693	35	37	− 2
Texas	.333	.763	27	27	0
Utah	.619	1.097	3	10	− 7
Vermont	.324	.744	29	32	− 3
Virginia	.242	.538	38	43	− 5
Washington	.490	1.120	13	8	+ 5
West Virginia	.489	1.095	14	11	+ 3
Wisconsin	.294	.985	30	17	+13
Wyoming	.646	1.490	2	1	+ 1
50 states and Washington, D.C.	.308	.742			

*Through state and local taxes.

SOURCE: *Financial Statistics of Institutions of Higher Education, 1967–68,* U.S. Department of Health, Education, and Welfare, Washington, D.C., 1970. *Statistical Abstract of the United States, 1969,* U.S. Department of Commerce, Bureau of the Census, Washington, D.C., 1969.

The tax base varies so greatly from state to state that it is also useful to look at the percent of state and local taxes spent on higher education (see Table 4). It should be noted that the ten states that pay in excess of 10 percent of state and local per capita taxes for higher education have, on the average, more than 86 percent of their total university and college students enrolled in public institutions. On the other hand, the ten states that pay less than 6 percent of per capita state and local taxes for public higher education enroll, on the average, only 60 percent of their total college and university students in public institutions (see Appendix A).

The above figures do not reflect state expenditures from state and local taxes made to private colleges and universities. States which place heavy reliance on their private colleges and universities have provided some financial support for those colleges. A comparison of Table 5, which includes these payments to private institutions, with Table 3 shows that these payments do improve somewhat the rankings for Pennsylvania, New York, and Florida. As discussed in more detail in Section 10, in the last few years some

TABLE 4
*Percent of per
capita taxes**
spent on public
higher education
(1967–68)*

State	Percent	Rank
Wyoming	12.01	1
West Virginia	11.43	2
North Dakota	11.30	3
Oregon	11.00	4
New Mexico	10.92	5
South Dakota	10.88	6
Kentucky	10.84	7
Washington	10.60	8
Louisiana	10.32	9
Arizona	10.22	10
California	9.92	11
Utah	9.91	12
Montana	9.55	13
Mississippi	9.47	14
Colorado	9.45	15
Illinois	9.39	16
Alaska	9.29	17
Iowa	9.24	18
Texas	9.22	19
Idaho	9.20	20
Kansas	9.00	21
Indiana	8.95	22
Michigan	8.87	23
Hawaii	8.78	24
Alabama	8.72	25
Arkansas	8.68	26
South Carolina	8.62	27
Wisconsin	8.55	28
Nebraska	8.52	29
Missouri	8.47	30
Georgia	8.18	31
North Carolina	8.04	32
Florida	7.91	33
Tennessee	7.76	34
Oklahoma	7.55	35
Rhode Island	7.46	36
Nevada	7.36	37
Vermont	6.62	38

State	Percent	Rank
Maryland	6.59	39
Virginia	6.37	40
Maine	5.99	41
New Hampshire	5.87	42
Minnesota	5.86	43
Delaware	5.72	44
Ohio	5.55	45
Connecticut	5.28	46
New York	5.14	47
Pennsylvania	5.11	48
Massachusetts	3.68	49
New Jersey	3.46	50
50 states	7.6	

*Includes state and local taxes.

SOURCE: *Financial Statistics of Institutions of Higher Education, 1967–68*, U.S. Department of Health, Education, and Welfare, Washington, D.C., 1970. *Statistical Abstract of the United States, 1969*, U.S. Department of Commerce, Bureau of the Census, Washington, D.C., 1969.

states have expanded their programs of aid to private institutions, and if figures were available to update Tables 3 and 5, state contributions to private institutions might have a more significant effect on state rankings. Inclusion of state aid for capital expenditures at private institutions would also modify the rankings.

Open-access policies

The requisites for effective open access are admission requirements under which all high school graduates or otherwise qualified adults are admissible to an appropriate geographically accessible college in the system at which either low or no tuition is charged for a student's first two years of postsecondary education.

State-by-state comparisons of the adequacy of open-access systems pose formidable problems. State tuition policies can be relatively easily obtained, but to assess the real impact of tuition on access, the state's policy and practice on financial aid programs must be considered as well. Minimum admission requirements can be obtained, but in practice an institution may use higher standards. Mileage calculations provide some measure of geographic accessibility, but differences in settings and transportation systems may make 10 miles an easy commutation in one state and difficult in another.

TABLE 5
Percent of per capita income spent* on all higher education (1967–68)

State	Percent	Rank
Wyoming	1.49	1
South Dakota	1.30	2
North Dakota	1.25	3
Arizona	1.22	4
New Mexico	1.19	5
Hawaii	1.13	6
Oregon	1.13	7
Washington	1.12	8
Louisiana	1.10	9
Utah	1.10	10
West Virginia	1.10	11
California	1.09	12
Montana	1.07	13
Colorado	1.06	14
Idaho	1.05	15
Iowa	1.00	16
Wisconsin	.99	17
Mississippi	.97	18
Kentucky	.95	19
Kansas	.92	20
Arkansas	.83	21
Michigan	.83	22
Indiana	.83	23
Alaska	.79	24
Alabama	.77	25
South Carolina	.77	26
Florida	.77	27
Texas	.77	28
Nebraska	.76	29
Illinois	.76	30
Nevada	.75	31
Vermont	.75	32
North Carolina	.74	33
Missouri	.74	34
Georgia	.73	35
Oklahoma	.73	36
Tennessee	.70	37

State	Percent	Rank
New York	.69	38
Rhode Island	.67	39
Minnesota	.67	40
Maryland	.62	41
Maine	.59	42
Virginia	.54	43
Delaware	.54	44
Pennsylvania	.52	45
New Hampshire	.50	46
Connecticut	.46	47
Ohio	.43	48
Massachusetts	.39	49
New Jersey	.31	50
50 states	.758	

*Through state and local taxes.

SOURCE: *Financial Statistics of Institutions of Higher Education, 1967–68,* U.S. Department of Health, Education, and Welfare, Washington, D.C., 1970. *Statistical Abstract of the United States, 1969,* U.S. Department of Commerce, Bureau of the Census, Washington, D.C., 1969.

The study recently completed by Warren W. Willingham (1) is the nearest approach to a systematic study of the varying accessibility of higher education in different parts of the nation. Willingham identifies "free-access colleges" as those which are generally nonselective in admission requirements and have tuition less than $400 a year. Willingham determined that approximately two-fifths of the United States population lives within commuting distance of free-access colleges (see Table 6). According to Willingham, states in the South and West are doing the best in making free-access colleges available. In the West, 51 percent of the population lives within commuting distance of a free-access college, and in the South, 50 percent. The percentages drop to 38 percent and 33 percent for the Northeast and Midwest, respectively.

It is possible to find fault with Willingham's definitions of commuting distance in particular areas or with his measure of nonselectivity. Furthermore, emphasis on tuition without reference to financial aid programs may lead to a distorted picture of the extent of economic barriers. Nonetheless, we believe that the Willingham study provides a valuable tool for state policy makers. States with a low proportion of their students within commuting distance of a

TABLE 6 *Free-access colleges by state (fall 1968)*

Regions and states	Population in millions (1967)	Number of colleges		Percent of population within commuting distance of free-access colleges*			
		Total	Free-access	Total	White	Black	Spanish surname†
Northeast	48.2	647	92	38	38	37	–
Connecticut	2.9	47	13	87	87	90	–
Maine	1.0	22	0	0	0	–	–
Massachusetts	5.4	105	13	52	53	25	–
New Hampshire	0.7	20	2	44	44	–	–
New Jersey	7.0	57	10	38	36	59	–
New York	18.3	206	34	36	38	23	36
Pennsylvania	11.6	155	16	25	24	41	–
Rhode Island	0.9	15	1	41	40	60	–
Vermont	0.4	20	3	41	41	–	–
South	61.4	821	312	50	50	52	–
Alabama	3.5	50	24	56	57	54	–
Arkansas	2.0	23	12	43	43	42	–
Delaware	0.5	6	2	35	35	44	–
D.C.	0.8	19	3	82	82	81	–
Florida	6.0	59	26	64	62	72	–
Georgia	4.5	56	14	30	33	24	–
Kentucky	3.2	47	17	52	51	69	–
Louisiana	3.7	27	15	48	49	47	–
Maryland	3.7	50	19	57	59	47	–
Mississippi	2.3	46	26	65	67	63	–
North Carolina	5.0	92	29	68	69	67	–
Oklahoma	2.5	36	16	31	31	26	–
South Carolina	2.6	52	12	56	58	53	–
Tennessee	3.9	55	16	41	39	52	–
Texas	10.9	113	54	38	37	43	40
Virginia	4.5	63	15	50	52	40	–
West Virginia	1.8	27	12	54	53	59	–
Midwest	55.1	740	193	33	33	39	–
Illinois	10.9	125	41	56	56	59	57
Indiana	5.0	52	0	0	0	0	–
Iowa	2.8	58	18	39	39	52	–
Kansas	2.3	50	21	43	42	59	–
Michigan	8.6	88	29	40	41	33	–

Regions and states	Population in millions (1967)	Number of colleges		Percent of population within commuting distance of free-access colleges*			
		Total	Free-access	Total	White	Black	Spanish surname†
Minnesota	3.6	54	21	29	30	24	–
Missouri	4.6	67	15	41	39	60	–
Nebraska	1.4	28	8	16	16	0	–
North Dakota	0.6	16	8	30	30	–	–
Ohio	10.5	116	7	12	12	19	–
South Dakota	0.7	16	3	12	12	–	–
Wisconsin	4.2	70	22	47	47	89	–
West	33.0	388	192	51	51	48	55
Alaska	0.3	10	8	31	31	–	–
Arizona	1.6	14	8	38	39	42	30
California	19.2	187	86	60	60	48	66
Colorado	2.0	29	15	42	41	58	48
Hawaii	0.7	11	5	48	48	–	–
Idaho	0.7	11	6	40	40	–	–
Montana	0.7	12	8	31	31	–	–
Nevada	0.4	2	0	0	0	0	–
New Mexico	1.0	16	8	22	24	38	16
Oregon	2.0	38	13	49	49	75	–
Utah	1.0	12	5	20	19	–	–
Washington	3.1	39	23	51	51	53	–
Wyoming	0.3	7	7	43	43	–	–
TOTAL U.S.	198.0	2,596	789	42	42	47	47

*Dash used when base too small for reliable estimate.
†Spanish surname: Mexican-Americans, Cubans, Puerto Ricans.
SOURCE: *Chronicle of Higher Education,* October 19, 1970, p. 5.

free-access college as determined by Willingham should evaluate carefully their higher education resources and policies in terms of open access.

A growing number of states provide open access to higher education through a network of open-door community colleges. Other states have open access through one or more state colleges or universities. But several states still maintain selective standards over the whole range of their public higher education institutions.

In its report *The Open-Door Colleges,* the Commission supports community colleges as an effective means for increasing accessibility of higher education to greater numbers of Americans.

The Commission recommends that:

1 All states, but particularly those with ratios below 70 percent, take steps to increase the percent of high school students who remain in high school and successfully complete the high school program.

2 States that rank low in terms of the proportion of students going on to higher education substantially increase their financial commitment to higher education.

3 State and local communities implement the Commission's recommendations for establishing 230 to 280 additional open-door community colleges as set forth in the Commission's report *The Open-Door Colleges.*

4 States showing a low proportion of their students within commuting distance of free-access colleges immediately undertake an evaluation of their higher education system to determine if, in fact, it lacks open access as a system and, if so, what steps need be taken to achieve reasonable open access.

7. The State and the Nonresident Student

Postsecondary students can and often do select their institutions without regard to state boundaries. In the fall of 1968, about one-sixth of all college and university students were enrolled in institutions outside their states of residence. In private institutions, out-of-state students constituted about one-third of total enrollment while nonresidents constituted only about one-tenth of total enrollment in public institutions.

Some states are heavy net exporters of students: Connecticut, Illinois, Maryland, New Jersey, and New York each exported at least 15,000 more students than they imported in 1968. Other states are heavy net importers of students: Colorado, District of Columbia, Indiana, Massachusetts, Michigan, Missouri, North Carolina, Tennessee, and Utah each had a net student import in excess of 15,000 in the fall of 1968 (see Appendix I).

POLICIES TOWARD NONRESIDENT STUDENTS The nonresident student seeking admission at a public institution is faced with several barriers: in most instances he will have to pay higher tuition and fees than the resident student; he often will have to meet more selective admission standards; and, increasingly, his enrollment may be subject to established quotas for nonresidents. All indications suggest that these barriers will increase over the next decade.

These restrictive policies are supported by the arguments that out-of-state students should not occupy space needed by resident students and that the already overburdened taxpayers of the state should not subsidize the college education of students of other states. For many years the first argument was based more on prospect than on actuality, but recent enrollment pressures have led to enrollment limits at several public institutions. Figures on per capita expenditures for public higher education tend to support the second argument. The average per capita expenditure for public higher education for the heavy net exporter states is less than half the average per capita expenditure for the net importer states.

Many educational leaders are concerned about the growth of restrictive policies. They cite several reasons for more liberal policies for admission of out-of-state students:

- Restrictions against nonresident students make it difficult to recruit nationally for the most able students for highly specialized graduate programs.

- Out-of-state students contribute to the diversity of the student body and therefore enhance the academic and extracurricular environment of the campus.

- The extension of educational opportunity is a concern of all states and it should not be artificially limited by state boundaries.

- Because few states are able to provide adequate postsecondary education in all fields, the introduction of a system of state barriers is detrimental to the residents of all states.

- Levels of existing or proposed federal assistance for certain graduate and professional programs support the elimination of nonresident tuition differentials for these programs.

With reference to graduate students, the reasons have been sufficiently compelling to lead to widespread use of tuition and fee waivers for highly able nonresident graduate students. But the reasons have not carried the general persuasiveness necessary to stem the tide of increasing restrictions against nonresident undergraduate students.

RESIDENCY CRITERIA Assuming the continuation and extension of nonresident restrictions, certain problems take on greater significance. Lack of uniformity in residence requirements among states could lead to situations in which a student would not qualify as a resident of any state. Furthermore, there may be little similarity in residence criteria of different institutions within the same state or between residence criteria for determining fee status at public institutions and for other purposes, such as voting. If the requirements for residency for educational purposes appear more restrictive than for other purposes or if the educational requirements are applied differentially, these policies are more vulnerable to constitutional questions of equal protection of the laws.

Perhaps more important is the fact that residency requirements as presently constructed are more restrictive than they need to be for the purposes for which they were originally intended. The original purpose would seem to have been to keep nonresidents from coming to the state solely for the purpose of obtaining an education, but some state requirements also define as nonresidents students from families who have moved recently for other than educational purposes.

To alleviate some of the problems described above resulting from nonresident policies, the Commission recommends that:

1 States, possibly working through the Education Commission of the States, carefully review their residence requirements and modify them if necessary for the purpose of granting immediate residence status to students whose families came to the state for other than educational reasons.

2 States, possibly working through the Education Commission of the States, cooperate for the purpose of developing relatively standard residence criteria and that each state review the implementation of requirements of its own institutions to insure similar application of the criteria among public institutions.

The Education Commission of the States has recently adopted a resolution recognizing the need for reform on this subject (see Appendix J).

INTERSTATE COOPERATION   A much higher degree of interstate cooperation is required if states are to take advantage of the opportunities afforded by interstate student migration. These opportunities are most evident at the graduate level. The very high costs of top quality graduate and professional instruction, particularly in medicine and in the sciences where complex laboratory equipment is essential, make it difficult for any one state to offer in its public institutions a complete range of graduate and professional curricula. Increasingly, high-cost graduate and professional instruction ought to be considered on a regional or a national basis rather than a state basis, with universities specializing in high-quality graduate offerings in particular disciplines. Reciprocity agreements do exist in some states. States involved in regional education compacts, such as the Southern Regional Education Board, the Western Interstate Commission for Higher Education, and the New England Board for Higher Education, have developed reciprocity agreements that enhance the educational programs of each of the states involved.

The development of use, on an exchange basis, of undergraduate institutions near the borders of contiguous states may work to the mutual benefit of these states. Insufficient attention seems to have been given to the possibility of reciprocity agreements involving undergraduate students.

The Commission's first Special Report recommended the establishment of a federal doctoral fellowship program with selection based upon demonstrated academic ability without reference to need. The Commission also recommended that institutions attended by doctoral fellowship recipients should receive a federal cost-of-education supplement.

To encourage the continued development of quality in graduate education at public institutions by permitting students of high ability to attend public institutions without reference to their residency, the Carnegie Commission recommends that:

1 The cost-of-education supplements accompanying the doctoral fellowships recommended in the Commission's first Special Report be available only to those institutions that charge the doctoral recipient a fee that is not affected by his residency status.

2 States consider carefully the adverse effects of enrollment limits at the graduate level for out-of-state students.

To take advantage of the opportunities afforded by interstate mobility of students, the Commission recommends that states enter into reciprocity agreements for the exchange of both undergraduates and graduate students in those situations where the educational systems of each of the states will be enhanced by such an exchange agreement.

Regional boards and the Education Commission of the States are excellent mechanisms for facilitating such agreements.

The Commission also suggests consideration of the possibility of developing a policy under which states would charge nonresident tuition fees only to students from states which are not undertaking their fair share of the task in supplying adequate student places for the nation's youth. Thus, a state might not charge any nonresident tuition if the student came from a state which showed a net import of students but would charge a nonresident tuition if the student came from a state that had substantial net exports over a number of years.

The special problems of state variations in tuition charges for nonresident medical students is discussed in the Commission's recent report, *Higher Education and the Nation's Health: Policies for Medical and Dental Education.* In that report, the Commission recommends that medical schools eliminate any tuition differentials or preferential admission provisions for resident students.

8. The State and Private Institutions

The more than 1,400 private universities and colleges in the nation, enrolling about one-fourth of all college and university students, are an important element in the nation's higher education system. Private institutions are those which are privately governed and whose operating income is largely derived from private or federal sources, and include independent or church-related two-year colleges, liberal arts colleges, technical colleges, professional schools, and universities.

For well over a hundred years almost all state governments have dealt at arm's length with private colleges and universities. Except for a few states which have a very low percentage of their students enrolled in public institutions, states have not directly and broadly subsidized the operation of private institutions. In the last few years, however, several states are reconsidering their roles vis-à-vis private colleges and universities.

IMPORTANCE OF THE PRIVATE SECTOR As shown earlier, relative enrollment in private higher education varies from state to state and has also varied substantially over time (see Map 1 and Figure 1). Until 1968, although the proportion of total students enrolled in private institutions had significantly declined, the number of students in private institutions continued to grow. In 1968 and 1969, however, not only had the proportion dropped, but the number of students enrolled in private institutions had also dropped. In 1970, the number of students enrolled in private institutions increased slightly, although the proportion again dropped.

In addition to the 1,400 private colleges and universities, many institutions also provided technical and vocational education. Conservative estimates place the number of private trade and vocational institutions at 7,000 with an enrollment of about 1.5 million.

63

Traditional distinctions between public and private institutions may be diminishing. Distinctions are now often based more on institutional type or on quality of the institution than on whether the institution is public or private. Major universities, whether public or private, tend to compete for the same students, for the same faculty, and for research grants from the same agencies. Although there are few public counterparts for the small private undergraduate liberal arts college, even this distinction may be fading somewhat as more public institutions experiment with undergraduate "cluster" colleges.

Student bodies in public institutions vary somewhat from those in private institutions, but the differences are sharply reduced if public institutions with high admissions standards are compared with private institutions with high admissions standards.

Endowment funds, which traditionally have been important to the private sector, have grown in significance at certain public universities. The average endowment per student at a private institution is still, however, more than six times as large as the average endowment per student at a public institution, but the importance of endowments in total income has declined for both types of institutions.

The sharp public-private dichotomy, undoubtedly reinforced over the years by divergent higher education association loyalties, is now rarely invoked by the private sector and tends to be ignored by others. For the most part, present federal higher education programs do not make material distinctions between public and private institutions except for prohibiting the use of public funds for sectarian purposes. The Carnegie Commission's first report on federal responsibility for higher education also assumed that federal programs should treat public and private institutions alike. Many state scholarships are available to students at both public and private colleges. Calling for full utilization of all higher education resources, recent state studies on private higher education have stressed that all colleges and universities, whether supported by public or private sources, function in the public interest and that graduates of private institutions benefit society, just as do the graduates of public institutions. A recent Oregon study took an additional step and asserted that there is no longer any purely "private" college or university (2).

Although distinctions between the private and public sector are insufficient to maintain a sharp dichotomy, there are still certain basic differences. The nation's private colleges and universities have an average enrollment of about one-third that of the average public institutions. Many private colleges have greater flexibility in determining and applying admission standards than do public colleges. All public institutions in a state account to some extent to their public through the state government, while each private institution in the state is subject to a different source of control. And the private institutions, while enjoying a greater freedom from government control, are at a serious disadvantage in most states in obtaining direct public financial support.

In many states, private colleges and universities, although proportionately small in enrollment, have served as buffers against excessive political control of state universities and colleges. The independent institution provides a yardstick against which degrees of governmental control can be measured, and it may serve as a basis for effectively resisting excessive control.

Many of the best private colleges have unique characters and special educational missions. Colleges with religious orientations can exist only as private institutions. Innovations can more easily be carried out at private institutions. The Antioch work-study program, the Goddard self-planned educational program, the first establishment of the Ph.D. degree in the United States at Yale, or the new "awareness" college at the University of Redlands, probably would have been more difficult to develop initially under the watchful eyes of state budget officers. Several recent experiments in public institutions, however, suggest that even the innovative approach is decreasingly unique to private colleges.

The high-quality private universities have provided excellent competition for major state universities. Today, the major national universities test their academic excellence against other major national universities without regard to whether such institutions are publicly or privately controlled.

Neither quantitative measures nor lists of distinctions tell the real importance of the private sector to American higher education. The presence of the private sector has added to the range of diversity and potential for experimentation in American higher education. Because of the interaction of public and private segments, higher education in the United States has been a more dynamic evolving force, and as a system, has avoided many of the major bureaucratic problems so frequently inherent in more centralized systems.

The Commission believes that there is continued need for a strong private sector in American higher education. The presence of the private sector extends diversity, provides a valuable dimension for developing quality, aids in protecting autonomy for all higher education, and fosters the type of institution which gives individual treatment to individual students.

The Commission recommends that states which do not presently have a strong private sector consider the desirability of making the equivalent of land grants to responsible groups who can demonstrate financial ability to operate new private institutions. Such grants should encourage groups to start new institutions or to open branches of existing well-established private institutions in the granting state.

Many observers today are predicting the demise of all but the more prestigious private institutions unless states provide financial support for private higher education.

FINANCIAL STATUS OF PRIVATE COLLEGES Increasingly, over the past few years, private higher education has called upon state governments to provide operating subsidies for the state's private colleges and universities. The argument for the subsidies is the continued need for private educational resources and the present tenuous financial status of private colleges and universities.

Preliminary results of a Carnegie-sponsored study on resources for higher education show that instructional costs per credit hour in private colleges and universities were greater than in public colleges and universities over the entire period from 1930 to 1967.

This finding is consistent with the conclusion reached in another study that "expenditures per student, as a rule, are higher in private than in public institutions," with the exception of Catholic liberal arts colleges (3).

Average faculty salaries in 1968–69 were higher at private independent universities than at public universities, but were somewhat lower at church-related universities and private four-year colleges, and substantially lower at private junior colleges. The percent of salary increases was lower at all private institutions than public institutions in 1968–69, but higher for the decade 1960–1970, as a whole. The range of salaries among private institutions, however, is broad. Eight of the ten universities paying the highest average professional salary were private.

In the period from 1959–60 to 1965–66, private institutions increased their physical plant per student by almost 50 percent, as compared to an increase of 12 percent for public institutions.

A Carnegie Commission study of college and university income from 1953 to 1966 provides a detailed comparison per student in public and private institutions for the nation and state by state. Figure 2 shows that, for the nation as a whole over the last 12 years, income per student in private institutions has risen much more rapidly than it has in public institutions. This is true regardless of whether or not income for organized research and auxiliary activities is included in total institutional income. In 1953–54, the per-student income in private institutions was higher than in public institutions in only 16 states. By 1966–67, this was true in 30 states.

In 1967–68, private colleges and universities received almost 40 percent of current fund income for all higher education institutions, but enrolled only 30 percent of total students enrolled in the fall of 1967.

These indices of relative affluence make it difficult to understand why private institutions are now seeking public subsidies on the basis of financial problems. There are several possible explanations for this seeming paradox:

1   Private institutions have greater expense for some purposes than do public institutions. They often, for example, incur significant expenditures in recruiting students, while public institutions rarely do. Furthermore, partly because of the higher tuition levels, private institutions must make a greater amount of student aid available. The 515 private institutions that belong to the Independent College Funds of America increased their scholarship grants seven-fold between 1956 and 1968. The percentage of their student bodies receiving financial assistance rose from 28 to 43 percent in the same period.

2   The average expenditures do not properly reflect the different per-student costs at various types of institutions. In many states, the large number of public junior colleges with low costs per student decreases the average for all public institutions in the state. The relatively higher proportion of graduate students in the student

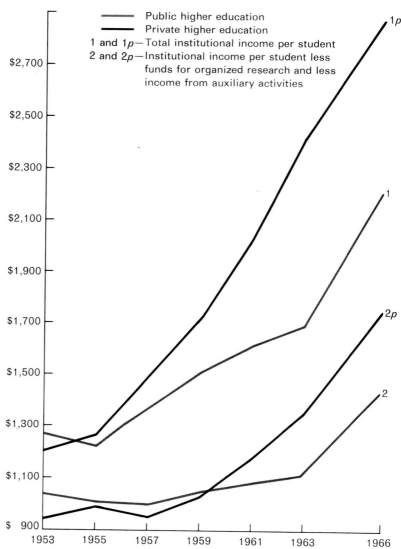

FIGURE 2
Institutional income per student

Public higher education
Private higher education
1 and 1*p*—Total institutional income per student
2 and 2*p*—Institutional income per student less funds for organized research and less income from auxiliary activities

mix at private universities may make private university per-student costs seem higher unless there is an adjustment for this difference.

3 To some extent, rising per-student costs in private institutions result from involuntary diseconomies of scale. As noted earlier, private institutions, on the average, are one-third the size of public institutions. A drop in enrollment in small colleges can have a large, and unplanned, effect on per-student costs. Conversely, rapid expansion in enrollment, such as that which occurred with the

influx of GI's after World War II, can lead to declines in per-student costs.

4 Both institutional income per student and expenditures per student have been computed with full-time-equivalent enrollment as the denominator. Since there is some evidence that several private institutions are able to maintain a persistence rate at least one and one-half times the persistence rate at many public institutions, the unit cost and income comparisons would be very different if the unit of measurement were degrees awarded rather than f.t.e. enrollment.

Cost comparisons between public and private institutions can be quite misleading. As mentioned above, gross per-student cost comparisons obscure a great range of differences among institutional types. Because the general pattern of institutional types differs significantly between the private and public sectors, it is not possible to obtain public-private cost comparisons for major portions of higher education. The traditional small private liberal arts college has no counterpart in public higher education. The comprehensive state colleges and the community colleges have few counterparts in private higher education. Perhaps only for major research and professional universities could meaningful cost comparisons be made. Even for these, however, there are important differences in treatment of public service functions and student services. Furthermore, the very things for which we most highly value private institutions—diversity, individual attention, quality, and innovation—are likely to result in higher per-student costs.

One other factor of great importance in explaining this seeming discrepancy is the lag in obtaining reliable financial data. In the studies on cost per student and costs per credit hour, the most recent data were four to five years old.

Studies utilizing more recent data on particular institutions or on all private colleges and universities in a state provide more convincing evidence of financial distress.

An article entitled "Private Colleges: A Question of Survival" appeared in *Fortune* magazine in October of 1967. The article predicted a combined annual deficit of $110 million for 20 of the nation's wealthiest private colleges by 1978.

Provost William Bowen of Princeton, in a study of the economics of private universities published by the Carnegie Commission, projected present trends in expenditures and revenue and concluded that a typical major private university would have a deficit of from $20 million to $28 million per year by 1975–76. He pointed out that a deficit of this size would not in fact be permitted to occur, but concluded that unless new sources of income were found, such institutions could no longer play any innovative roles or maintain for very long their past standards of performance (4).

Reports from various state studies of private higher education echo these predictions of financial distress.

A 1967 study of private higher education in Missouri warned that "Private colleges face serious demands as they seek to maintain their present stability and to realize their plans for growth . . . to maintain health, these colleges will have to find new and substantial sources for current operating as well as for capital development" (5).

The Texas study states that "several independent colleges have been operating under deficit conditions for at least two years, and there is no independent college in Texas which has an endowment large enough to permit it to face the future without real financial concern" (6).

The New York study "found evidence of serious need, but not of impending catastrophe" (7), but the letter of transmittal cast some doubt on this conclusion by stating, "One of our more important findings is that no one really knows precisely the exact financial condition of New York's private colleges and universities." The Commission concluded, however, that a modest amount of public aid was required to assure the vigorous health of the private sector for the forseeable future.

The Illinois Commission found that private institutions in that state were operating with a small surplus in their educational and general funds and their auxiliary enterprise accounts. But the Commission argued that "This 'black' figure, however, actually disguises a serious underlying deficiency, one which, unless repaired, can only become worse. The surplus is achieved at the cost of relatively low faculty salaries, a significant amount of deferred maintenance, and inadequate library development" (8). The Illinois report concluded that "if this trend continues, deficits in the private sector will be the general rule in the relatively near future" (ibid., p. 25).

Studies of private higher education in Indiana and Massachusetts completed this year are more specific about the financial crisis of private institutions. The Massachusetts study predicted that "private higher education in Massachusetts will face deficits on the order of $50 million by 1975–76, and perhaps two to three times that amount by 1980–81 (9). In Indiana, almost half of that state's private colleges and universities reported an operating deficit in 1968–69, and the study projected a deficit for Indiana's private sector of $39 million by 1974–75 (10).

A recently completed Carnegie Commission study (11) of the financial status of 41 public and private colleges and universities suggests that many colleges and universities, both public and private, are either experiencing "financial difficulty" or are "headed for financial trouble." The 41 colleges studied included 18 public institutions, of which 1 was determined to be "in financial difficulty" and 9 were "headed for financial trouble." Of the 23 private colleges, 10 were considered to be "in financial difficulty" and 9 were "headed for financial trouble." Only 4 private institutions were considered not in financial trouble while 8 public institutions were put in this category.

The evidence is growing that higher education in general is facing a period of financial stringency, and that the stringency has already hit more private than public institutions. The differential impact of this "new depression" may be due in part to traditional differences in revenue sources for public and private institutions.

SOURCES OF REVENUE Some participants in the controversy over the degree of the private college financial crisis suggest that the alleged crisis results from the availability of better techniques for projecting costs than for projecting income. Institutional income estimates are complicated by many factors that are either difficult or impossible to reflect in such projections.

Traditional sources of income for colleges and universities are: (1) tuition and other student fees, (2) government support, (3) gifts and bequests, and (4) income on invested funds. High interest rates in recent years have made relatively good returns on investment possible, almost regardless of investment management skill. There is no question that endowments will require better management in the future if past yield rates are to be maintained or improved. The recent Ford Foundation study on university endowment funds concluded that most colleges and universities should invest their endowment funds more boldly and widely (12).

According to the Council for Financial Aid to Education, there was a sharp acceleration in the growth of voluntary support of higher education in 1967–68 as compared to the two previous years. Of the various sources of voluntary support, alumni assistance appears to be the fastest growing and most stable. The financial problems of higher education will not be greatly eased by sharp rises in alumni contributions, however, since these account for only 10 percent of total current-fund income.

Public institutions have traditionally relied heavily upon the third source of funds, government support. Private institutions, in recent years, have received increased support from federal sources —from 15 percent of total income in 1957 to 25 percent in 1966. The federal support, much of it concentrated in the major private universities, however, has been largely for research support. If federal research grants are excluded from federal support and also from total income, the increase in federal support to private institutions from 1957 to 1966 was from 1 to 5 percent of income. During the same period, support for private institutions from state and local government increased from 1.6 to 1.9 percent of total income.

The fourth source of income, tuition and other student fees, has been relied upon heavily by private institutions. It is clear that many private institutions are not able to increase tuition as rapidly as they might feel necessary to meet rising expenses. Some small private colleges are reluctant to raise tuition because they fear it would lead to drops in enrollment. For certain prestige private colleges, which receive three or four times as many applications as available places, market conditions would seem ideal to raise fees as high as necessary. But education is not a commodity which can be priced solely with reference to economic forces in the market. Recent efforts to increase tuition at private institutions have resulted in student strikes, leading in some instances to fee increases smaller than originally announced. For most students, education is purchased over a number of years, and at any one time a college is dealing with a large percentage of continuing purchasers rather than a group of new purchasers. Tuition increases might be easier to achieve if all purchasers were new purchasers at any given time.

Furthermore, private colleges have made great strides in recent years to reduce the social stratification in the student bodies of their institutions. If the nation is to meet its goals of equality of educational opportunity, it is necessary for private as well as public institutions to increase the number of students from low socio-

economic families in their student bodies. To do so, however, requires increased allocation of institutional funds for financial aid
for these students. Costs for this purpose at private colleges have
risen more rapidly than almost all other institutional costs. Increases in tuition would also increase this expense item.

9. Public and Private Tuition Levels

Low tuition in public higher education is usually credited with the ever-increasing popularity of public institutions. Until the last few decades, few public institutions had the prestige of the best private colleges and universities. But the low cost of tuition made it possible for vast numbers of students to attend public colleges who would not otherwise have been able to obtain a college education. The individual's gain was also the nation's gain.

But critics of the low-tuition principle are becoming more numerous, and there are signs that they are also becoming more effective. In a recent Carnegie Commission study of legislative attitudes, approximately half of the legislators interviewed were in favor of increasing tuition fees. A recent survey of state colleges and universities showed 174 out of 258 institutions had increased tuition for the 1969–70 academic year.

The proponents and opponents of low tuition engage in a never-ending dialogue, a dialogue in which some of the participants base their arguments on such different values and start from such different assumptions that a satisfactory resolution of their conflict seems unlikely, if not impossible.

The opponents of tuition increases argue that:

1   Education benefits society by training a citizenry capable of managing and adapting to change; by producing an informed electorate; by graduating employable, productive, high-level manpower for the labor force; and by stimulating the arts and humanities. Since society as a whole benefits, the general taxpayers should bear the tuition cost. The student is investing enough in his own future when he pays subsistence costs and fees and sacrifices earnings while in school.

2   Neither state nor federal scholarship programs have been adequate at any time in the past (nor are they at present) to make it possible for all qualified students from low-income families to attend college. Increased tuition will make these programs even more inadequate than they are now.

3   Any tuition in public education is class biased. It gives preferential access to students from socioeconomic groups having higher ability to pay. Thus, imposing higher tuition will result in a change in the composition of the student body in university and state college systems which will carry us farther away from our goal of equal educational opportunity.

4   Students who have gone to college earn higher incomes and thus pay higher income taxes—more than offsetting subsidies granted through low tuition.

The proponents of increased tuition argue that:

1   A university graduate realizes substantial private income benefits from higher education. Therefore, he should be willing to invest in his future by meeting at least a part of the cost of his education through tuition payments.

2   The present system of financing public higher education is regressive, putting a larger burden, in relation to benefit derived, on the low-income groups. Financing a larger portion of the cost through tuition will result in a less regressive financing pattern.

3   Obtaining a smaller proportion of its total budget from the state will increase diversity of funding for the institution, making possible greater assurance of institutional independence.

4   Increased tuition closer to the actual cost of education may provide for a more efficient allocation of resources.

5   Putting more of the burden of the costs of education on students may reduce taxpayer concern with student unrest.

6   Unless public institutions increase their tuition, private colleges will be priced out of the market.

7   Higher tuition at public institutions would result in more effective competition between public and private institutions and thus make for improved quality and greater diversity.

8   Tuition is an additional source of revenue badly needed by public institutions.

Figure 3 compares public to private tuition levels over the period from 1928 to 1968. The public-to-private ratio at colleges and universities (exclusive of two-year colleges) ranged from 1 to 2.57 in 1939–40, to 1 to 4.36 in 1963–64; and for 1968 was 1 to 4.13. For two-year colleges the change in ratio in recent years was more dramatic. In 1957, the ratio of tuition of public to private two-year institutions was 1 to 4.77; by 1967 it had climbed to 1 to 7.16 (see Figure 4).

In determining the marked influence on enrollment of changes in relative levels of public and private tuition, ratios may not be as

FIGURE 3   *Tuition rates at public and private four-year institutions for selected years (1927–1967)*

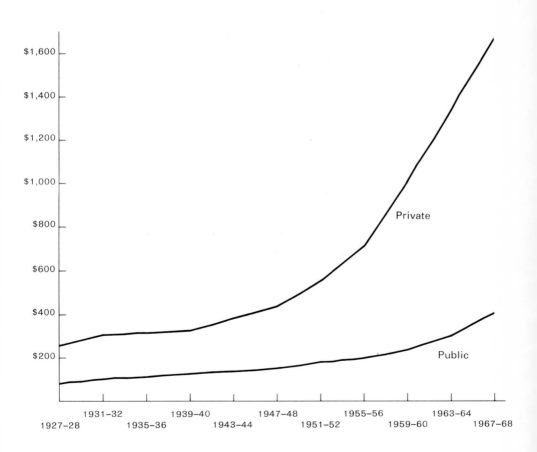

FIGURE 4
*Ratio of tuition
levels at public
and private
two-year
institutions for
selected years
(1957–1967)*

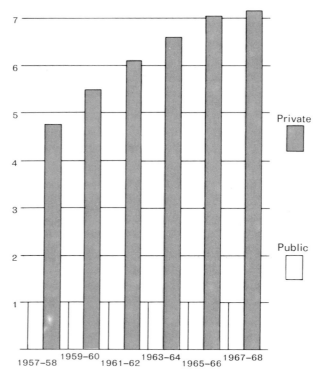

significant as the actual dollar gap. A public tuition of $100 compared with a private tuition of $400 does not have the same impact on selection of institutions as would a public tuition of $800 and a private tuition of $3,200. In both, the ratio is 1 to 4, but the $2,400 gap in the second instance makes it much more likely that the public institution will be selected. Figure 5 shows the change in actual dollar gap between public and private tuition levels.

Clearly the growing dollar gap has increased the proportion of public college enrollment. The Texas study views this gap with considerable alarm:

As the gap between public and private college tuition rates continues to increase, it becomes more and more difficult for a student to choose the independent college. Because more than half the educational and general income for the private institution comes from tuition and fees, drops in enrollment are especially alarming. . . . First year enrollments in the private senior colleges and universities have declined numerically for the last two years. . . . When the margin of financial stability is slight, the effect of a drop in enrollment can be almost catastrophic (6, pp. 39, 41).

SENSITIVITY
OF TUITION
LEVELS A further difficulty in solving tuition problems is that tuition be-
haves like other prices only in a very general way. Tuition levels are
often relatively insensitive to changes in the economy. Figure 6
compares increases in public and private tuition levels with increases in the consumer price index and disposable per capita personal income.

In the period from 1935 to 1968, disposable per capita income
increased at an annual rate of 5.6 percent, while public tuition
increased at the rate of 3.9 percent and private tuition at 5.2 percent
annually. If only the period from 1960 to 1968 is considered, however, the annual rate of increase for both public (6.4 percent) and
private tuition (6.6 percent) has been greater than that for per
capita disposable income (5.3 percent).

It would seem that tuition could certainly rise as fast as disposable per capita personal income. Because of the relative income
elasticity of demand for higher education, tuition could even rise
somewhat more rapidly than disposable income.

FIGURE 5 *Ratio of tuition levels at public and private four-year institutions for selected years
(1927–1967)*

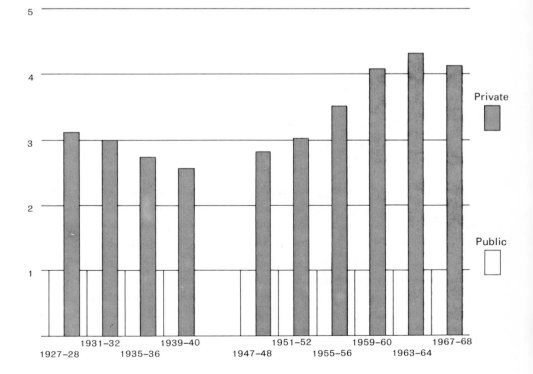

FIGURE 6
*Comparison
of increases
in tuition,
income, and
prices*
*(1931–1940 =
100)*

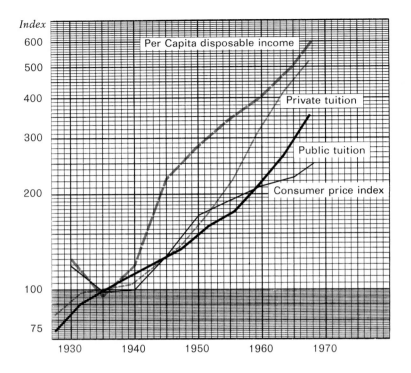

The failure of tuition trends to follow closely the consumer price index benefits institutions in a time of deflation but may put them at a serious disadvantage in periods of rapid inflation such as the present, since educational costs have tended to rise faster than consumer prices generally. This tendency may not be as marked in the next decade since the projected relationship between supply and demand for college faculty suggests that faculty salaries, which constitute a large component of total costs, will not rise as rapidly as they have in the past.

**TUITION
POLICY AND
EQUALITY OF
EDUCATIONAL
OPPORTUNITY** It would hardly be desirable to increase public tuition levels for the sole purpose of narrowing the public-private tuition gap. But this pressure, combined with growing concern by the taxpayers that the subsidies to public higher education are becoming much too burdensome, has set the stage for recent drives to increase tuition substantially. The impact of such increases on equal educational opportunity should be carefully considered.

The College Scholarship Service (CSS) estimates that no contribution toward college expense can be expected from a family with two dependent children which has an annual income of less than

$4,410. The U.S. Bureau of the Census estimates that about one-tenth of all families in relevant age groups and with dependent children in the nation receive an income below this level. For a family with two dependent children and an annual income of $8,000, the CSS estimates that a family contribution of $800 per year toward college expenses can be expected. Approximately two-fifths of the nation's families with dependent children in this category fall below this income level. Some have less than two dependent children, but many have more. The U.S. Office of Education estimates that the average cost of subsistence at public institutions in 1968–69 was $835; thus, the $800 contribution would be just enough to cover subsistence costs at public institutions without allowance for any tuition payments. It would appear, therefore, that children from at least 20 million families will experience increased financial disadvantage with every rise in tuition at public colleges and universities. These figures are quite conservative. The U.S. Bureau of Labor Statistics lower budget for an urban family of four was $6,567 in 1969 (13).

It is true that there would be no reason to forgo the ability of many to pay if the economic disadvantage of low-income families were offset with adequate student aid programs. At the present time, however, student aid programs at both the state and federal levels are inadequate.

STATE SCHOLARSHIP PROGRAMS Nineteen states have general programs of assistance for undergraduate students enrolled in both public and private institutions. These programs are restricted to residents and, in most instances, financial-need tests are established to determine the amount of the grant. Originally, most of the programs benefitted only those needy students among the most able students in the state as determined by test scores of high school records. More recently, 10 of these states (California, Illinois, Iowa, Michigan, Minnesota, New Jersey, New York, Oregon, Pennsylvania, and Wisconsin) have added non-competitive programs designed to aid needy students without competitive selection on the basis of ability.

In some of these noncompetitive programs, awards are limited to tuition and fees. In most of the others, the maximum amount of the award would permit inclusion of funds for subsistence only if the student attended a low-tuition public institution.

All the state programs combined provide some financial aid to about a half million students, less than one-tenth of all undergraduates in the nation, and, it is estimated, about one-fifth of those undergraduate students who could demonstrate financial need.

Table 7 summarizes the appropriations, average grants, and numbers of students aided for each of the state programs.

In its report *Quality and Equality,* issued in December 1968, and in the supplement to that report issued in June 1970, the Commission outlined an improved federal program for student aid. Ideally, state and federal programs should be designed to complement each other with the combined programs covering all aspects of the student's financial need. Since the proportion of enrollment in private institutions varies greatly from state to state, and tuition levels, both public and private, also vary greatly among the states, it would seem reasonable for the state to make grants to students for tuition. State policy is responsible both for the amount of public higher education available and also for the levels of public tuition. The federal government, however, is the better agency for covering student subsistence costs, which are relatively uniform across the nation.

PUBLIC IN-STITUTIONAL TUITION DIF-FERENTIALS Present average tuitions at four-year public institutions are almost three times as high as those at two-year public institutions. This differential is apparently based on the generally held assumption that quality — and therefore costs — are higher at four-year institutions, and thus tuition also should be higher. In states with both a university system and a college system, the same assumption about relative costs at different educational levels leads to higher tuition levels at the university.

This tuition practice results in greater inequality of educational opportunity for those students who are financially disadvantaged. The high-ability student from a high-income family can go to a university with high academic standards. But a high-ability student from a low-income family, faced with rising public university tuitions, will increasingly have no choice but a public community college. Even a massive grant program probably would not offset this disadvantage altogether, because the presence of low-tuition public community colleges tends to be an important element in setting the maximum levels of grants. Nor would greatly expanded loan programs be likely to offset this disadvantage since many young students are reluctant to borrow in the early stages of their college programs.

If education of freshmen and sophomores at a university actually

TABLE 7
Summary of
all state
comprehensive
undergraduate
grant programs
(competitive and
noncompetitive)
for residents of
the state to
attend either
public or
nonpublic
colleges or
universities* (for
1969–70)

State	Total dollars appropriated	Number of awards	Average award	Ratio of number of awards to number of 18- to 21-year-olds
California	$ 12,288,475	14,680	$837	.010
Connecticut	877,500	1,440	609	.008
Illinois	26,000,000	38,475	676	.055
Indiana	3,080,000	6,550	470	.019
Iowa	1,762,500	2,275	775	.013
Kansas	150,000	409	367	.003
Maine	61,000	150	407	.002
Maryland	2,900,000	7,250	400	.026
Massachusetts	2,000,000	3,000	667	.009
Michigan	12,500,000	24,030	526	.041
Minnesota	775,000	1,293	603	.005
New Jersey	11,850,000	26,658	445	.060
New York	58,800,000	263,000	224	.230
Oregon	815,400	6,961	117	.051
Pennsylvania	51,900,000	77,400	671	.108
Rhode Island	1,500,000	2,000	750	.032
Vermont	1,099,255	2,100	523	.079
West Virginia	175,000	625	280	.005
Wisconsin	2,950,000	9,510	350	.035
TOTALS	$191,484,130	487,806	$393	.066

*Source for first three columns is an unpublished paper entitled *An Examination of State Efforts in Removing Financial Barriers to Postsecondary Education* by Joseph D. Boyd. The last column is based on calculations by the Carnegie Commission staff.

In addition to the state programs included in Mr. Boyd's table, there is also a newly established Instructional Grants Program in Ohio providing up to $900 to needy students attending private institutions and up to $300 for those attending public institutions. In 1970–71, Ohio appropriated $8.5 million for this program.

does cost more than at a state college or community college, then even the negative impact on equal educational opportunity might not be sufficient to warrant reconsideration of the traditional fee differentials. Average student costs at a university are clearly higher than at a state college or a junior college when these costs are derived by dividing total expenditures by total enrollment. Further refinements in costing — such as relative weightings for graduate and undergraduate students; elimination of organized research; and adjustment for differences in auxiliary enterprises, administrative cost patterns, and financial aid patterns — narrow this differential considerably. There is reason to believe that a more refined cost accounting approach would show a quite different cost relationship than that ordinarily assumed today. Freshmen and sophomore classes in universities are often large, and part of the teaching of freshmen and sophomores is frequently carried on by teaching assistants; junior college classes tend to be smaller and are usually taught by full-fledged members of the faculty. It is therefore conceivable that a sophisticated cost analysis could show the same or even a lower cost for freshmen and sophomores at a university than at a junior college.

While it may be desirable in the long run to establish a tuition system based on actual cost differentials, cost analyses of the sort required to establish such a system are not now available. Even if such analyses were available, there is no assurance that our present cost relationships are desirable. Among the many suggestions for educational reform in higher education is the suggestion that we should reverse our apparent present tendency to spend more on upper-division students and less on lower-division students. It is argued that the first two years are the crucial years in developing the student's potential for further education, providing a solid basis for later study, and shaping his attitude toward higher education. Unless adequate resources are devoted to educating the student at the point of entry to higher education, he may never become an upper-division student.

Long-range policies on tuition must await intensive study of the role of tuition in financing higher education, full exploration of the potential of obtaining additional revenue from other sources, and greater understanding of and a rationale for determining appropriate public and private shares of the burden for financing higher education. The Carnegie Commission has undertaken studies on certain aspects of these questions. The work done to date indicates that the pricing of higher education may be one of the most difficult aspects of the whole range of questions involved in financing higher education, and one which has social and political implications far beyond what might be viewed as immediate economic implications.

In the short run, therefore, it is imperative to avoid responses to immediate and extreme pressures which would in any way make it difficult to adopt the best long-range tuition policies. Undoubtedly, states faced with an increasing burden of heavy subsidies to public higher education will feel that it is necessary to increase public tuition rates to some extent.

Increases in public tuition rates do not in themselves suggest abandonment of the low public-tuition principle. Tuition levels could be much higher than they were 50 years ago and still be considered "low" in relation to today's level of earnings. It is the rate of increase in relation to per capita income, rather than the fact of increase, which is significant in determining appropriate tuition policy.

The Commission recommends that states and public institutions that find it necessary to increase tuition and other required instructional fees, not increase such fees at a rate higher than the rate at which per capita personal disposable income rises, except that institutions which have kept their fees unusually low for many years may find it necessary to exceed this rate in initial increases.

If private institutions held their tuition increases to a rate somewhat less than the rate of increase in personal disposable income, the present gap in public and private tuition could be narrowed at least to the historic rate of about 1:3. Appropriation of some state funds to aid private colleges would make the slower rise of tuition possible.

The nation's equality of educational opportunity goal should not be jeopardized by adoption of tuition policies which do not realistically take into consideration existing levels of financial aid. As shown earlier, states have been traditionally slow in adopting adequate programs of student financial aid. The Commission's proposals for expanded federal opportunity grants and work-study programs contained in its first report, *Quality and Equality,* if implemented, would improve the situation greatly. But federal aid by itself would not be adequate. The Commission's proposals for federal aid include one feature designed to draw forth greater amounts of state support for student aid—the proposal for supplementary matching grants.

Nor can the federal program take into account variations in tuition levels among states or differing levels of availability of public education with its lower tuition levels in the several states. As mentioned earlier, tuition grants seem to be an appropriate feature for a state student aid program. Noncompetitive tuition grant programs, which recognize the need for higher grants to needy students attending colleges, have recently been established in Iowa, Michigan, New Jersey, and Wisconsin. The Commission believes that this type of program is a step in the right direction but would endorse broader tuition grant programs encompassing both public and private institutions. (For a description of the Iowa program, see Appendix K.)

The Commission recommends that states establish a program of tuition grants for both public and private institutions to be awarded to students on the basis of financial need. Only after establishment of a tuition grants program should states consider raising tuition levels at public institutions. To avoid upward pressures on private tuition from such grants, states would need to set a maximum tuition grant.

A basic goal for any long-range policy should be to have selection of institution depend upon the academic ability and talents of the student, rather than upon his economic ability to pay. A policy of free or nominal tuition for the first two years would encourage students who are interested in short-term technical and vocational education to complete their work. It would also encourage students who may not be highly motivated toward additional education to have some higher education experience so that they can better evaluate the benefits of continuing their education into the third year. Marked differences in tuition rates among the higher education segments of the state can increase social stratification in the postsecondary education system of the state.

The Commission recommends that no tuition or very low tuition be charged for the first two years in public institutions including community colleges, state colleges, and universities.

10. Public Funds for Private Higher Education

Recognition of the contributions of private colleges and universities to higher education, and concern for their ability to survive, have led some states to provide public funds for private higher education and have prompted several other states to consider seriously taking this step.

FORMS OF AID *Various tax preferences or exemptions* constitute the most universal form of aid to private institutions by state and local governments. In most states, private institutions are exempt from property taxes on any property used for educational purposes. Over the history of American higher education, foregone taxes have constituted and continue to constitute a substantial public contribution to private colleges and universities. States with income taxes also generally provide deductions for contributions to nonprofit educational institutions, and the states of Indiana and Michigan have recently enacted tax credit legislation under which individuals are permitted to claim credit against their taxes for contributions to educational institutions.

State scholarship programs also provide an indirect form of aid to private institutions. Most states with scholarship and grant programs provide for use of these funds at private as well as public institutions. It is estimated that in excess of $150 million of state-funded scholarships and grants was received in 1969–70 by students attending private colleges and universities.

Merger of a private institution into the public system is sometimes spoken of as a technique for aiding a particular private college or university. In the last decade some 50 institutions were merged into state systems. But the technique of merger cannot qualify as a form of aid. In those instances in which merger is advisable, it must be viewed as a technique for expanding public higher education rather than as a way to preserve private higher education. While the merged institution is assured participation in the state's public higher education expenditures, it becomes a part of the state public system subject to state control and is likely to lose any special characteristics it had as a private institution. The Commission opposes merger as a device to aid private institutions.

Contractual arrangements with private institutions have been used as a way of providing public funding for certain programs at private institutions without drastically affecting the organizational structure of the institution. For years the Colleges of Agriculture, Home Economics, and Veterinary Medicine and the School of Industrial and Labor Relations at Cornell have been publicly supported units of a private university. This support was granted under broad contractual arrangements.

Another form of contractual support is on a per-student basis for specific programs, often in the health sciences. Florida pays the University of Miami, a private institution, $6,500 for each Florida student enrolled in its medical school. Alabama and New York have similar arrangements. South Carolina makes contractual payments to private colleges on a per-student basis for teacher training programs.

Under the contractual arrangements administered by the Southern Regional Education Board, the Western Interstate Commission on Higher Education, and the New England Board of Higher Education, some 25 states have made payments through the regional agency for education of their residents at private institutions in other states.

Other states are showing interest in the contractual approach. The Illinois Commission to Study Non-Public Higher Education, which issued its report in March 1969, made a recommendation for "establishment of a fund for contracts with private institutions, individually or in consortium for special services or for performance of other tasks to meet state needs economically and efficiently" (8, p. 53).

Direct grants in the form of operating subsidies to selected institutions because of their value to the state higher education system have been made for some years by Pennsylvania. Wisconsin voted funds for the first time in 1969 to a private medical school, the College of Medicine at Marquette University. And in 1970 a subsidy of $1.5 million was voted by Ohio to Case Western Reserve Medical School.

General-formula institutional grants are grants to an institution to be used for general educational purposes, with the total amount of the grant based on a specified sum for each student enrolled, or each degree conferred, or other unit of measure related to the total size of the institution. Last year, the New York legislature adopted a program of general-formula institutional grants. Implementing the major recommendations of the Select Committee on the Future of Private and Independent Higher Education, the legislation provided that private nonsectarian colleges and universities receive annual grants of $400 for each undergraduate degree granted and $2,400 for each graduate degree. In the first year of this program, over $200 million were channeled to some 50 private institutions.

The Illinois Commission recommended a program of general-formula institutional grants to private institutions. Institutional grants were to be based upon the number of state scholarship and grant recipients enrolled in each institution and the number of all other full-time-equivalent undergraduate students enrolled (8, pp. 46, 47).

The *special-formula institutional grant* uses a somewhat different approach. In this type of grant, the funds may be used for general educational purposes, but the total amount of the grant is determined by how well the institution is meeting some special state goal. For example, to encourage greater equality of opportunity, a subsidy could be given for each student enrolled from a low-income family or holding a grant based on financial need as we recommended in *Quality and Equality;* or, to encourage better utilization of existing facilities, private institutions could be given a subsidy for each additional student over some base-year enrollment figure. Although the grants are actually administered under contractual arrangements, grants to Connecticut's private institutions are based on the latter type of special purpose formula: Connecticut pays to the private institutions 25 percent of current tuition (provided current tuition is less than the state's comparable cost of education) for each additional Connecticut student enrolled over a certain base year with the payments to be used for any educational purpose of the institution.

Limited purpose or categorical grants are funds granted to the institution for particular purposes, such as construction of academic facilities, dormitories, or improvement of faculty salaries. State construction grants to private universities and colleges are rare. Maryland has made such grants for several years, but since the 1966 decision holding certain of its grants unconstitutional, the grants have been limited to schools that can be clearly determined to be nonsectarian.

Illinois and New York have both made matched fund construction grants to health science schools. The Illinois Commission recommendations include a proposal for construction grants, as do the Pennsylvania Master Plan proposals.

State aid to private institutions for construction has most often been in the form of enabling institutions to borrow money for construction of educational facilities for self-financing corporations which issue tax-exempt bonds. Connecticut, Illinois, Massachusetts, Michigan, New Hampshire, New Jersey, New York, Ohio, Pennsylvania, South Carolina, and Vermont all have programs of this type.

New York has provided funds to endow chairs for distinguished professors at both public and private institutions. Ohio is considering categorical grants to improve college and university libraries. Pennsylvania has a long history of public aid to private institutions employing grants that feature many of the forms mentioned above. Over the last several years, between 15 and 25 private institutions received state aid. Two of these institutions, Temple University and the University of Pittsburgh, are, for certain purposes, considered a part of the state's education system and receive substantial state support but continue to operate as private corporations. Both Temple University and the University of Pittsburgh receive grants for general maintenance, tuition reduction supplements, and special appropriations for certain schools. The state also makes general maintenance grants and grants for special schools to the University of Pennsylvania and to several other professional and technical colleges. Such state grants on a selective basis for educational programs not adequately available through the state's public educational system seem entirely appropriate. Few other states would have the same pattern of characteristics in its educational system leading to a grant program of this type. But the principle involved, aiding those elements of the private system needed to augment the state's public system, could be applied in any state.

Table 8 summarizes some of the major programs of direct aid by states to private institutions. As the table clearly shows, such programs have increased in recent years.

In its first report, *Quality and Equality,* the Commission's proposals for aid to institutions made several forms of aid available to both public and private colleges. Many of the proposals called for categorical grants, such as construction funds, library and technological grants, and special program grants. The proposed cost-of-education supplements for doctoral fellows and holders of opportunity grants would be a special-formula institutional grant in which selection of the institutions to receive the grants is largely determined by students in particular categories.

Adoption of the Commission's recommendations for new levels of federal responsibility for higher education would undoubtedly re-

TABLE 8 *State grants and educational contract payments to private colleges and universities[a] for alternate fiscal years 1959-60 through 1969-70 (in thousands of dollars)*

State	1959-60	1961-62	1963-64	1965-66	1967-68	1969-70
Alabama[b]			635	790	590	590
Florida[c]		974	990	1,273	1,343	330
New York[d]	13,742	14,854	18,143	20,860	25,208	51,781
Ohio[e]						1,500
Pennsylvania[f]	15,691	17,889	23,932	40,513	76,826	101,701
Vermont[g]		114	124	40	40	40

[a] Does not include appropriations for capital expenditures.

[b] Alabama's grants are to Tuskegee Institute, Marion Institute, and Walker County Junior College.

[c] Florida's grants represent a subsidy ($3,500 prior to 1965-66, $4,500 thereafter) for each Florida student enrolled in the medical school of the private University of Miami.

[d] New York's grants are for colleges in the areas of agriculture, home economics, veterinary medicine, and industrial and labor relations, operated by Cornell University and in ceramics at Alfred University. The 1969-70 figure includes over $20 million for aid to private institutions under its newly adopted program of grants based on a general formula.

[e] Ohio's grant consists of a subsidy for the medical school of private Case Western Reserve University.

[f] Pennsylvania makes substantial grants to two state-related institutions operated as private corporations (the University of Pittsburgh and Temple University) and to the private University of Pennsylvania, as well as to certain private specialized schools in the health sciences, art, music, law, and technical fields.

[g] Vermont grants for operating expenses to private institutions are to Middlebury College and Norwich University in earlier years and to only Norwich University in the last three entries.

SOURCE: M. M. Chambers, *Higher Education in the Fifty States,* The Interstate Printers and Publishers, Inc., Illinois, 1970, pp. 27-28, 92-93, 262-264, 292-293, 322-325, and 350.

duce the financial distress of many private institutions to a state of mild discomfort.

Even with this aid, some private colleges will require additional state aid, either direct or indirect, if they are to continue as a part of the state's higher education resources. This is true particularly of small and lesser-known liberal arts colleges, colleges founded for Negroes, and junior colleges. If public aid is granted to these private institutions, careful consideration must be given to the constitutional and political problems inherent in grants to private institutions.

CONSTITU-TIONAL AND POLITICAL FEASIBILITY The Constitution of the United States prohibits Congress from making any laws "respecting an establishment of religion" and, through the Fourteenth Amendment this restriction is extended to the states. Efforts to interpret this restriction have led to much litigation, and the guidelines resulting from the cases have not always been clear. In *Horace Mann v. The Board of Public Works* (1966), the Court held that ". . . Hood, although it is a church-related school, may constitutionally receive state grants. It cannot be said to be 'sectarian' in a legal sense or to a degree that renders the grant invalid under the first amendment. The college's stated purposes in relation to religion are not of a fervent, intense or passionate nature, but seem to be based largely upon its historical background. Thus, the primary purpose of the grant to Hood College was not to aid or support religion." The Mann case declared unconstitutional, however, a grant to a college affiliated with the Methodist Church, all of whose presidents had been Methodist ministers, whose students may become interested in religion for the first time while attending the college, whose campus is made available to Methodist organizations, and whose stated purpose is to provide the best in higher education "within the framework and emphasis of the verities and values of our Christian faith." The Mann case also held unconstitutional two grants to Catholic colleges holding that grants "in a legal and constitutional sense (showed) a purpose to use the state's coercive power to aid religion."[1]

Litigation is still pending concerning the legality of construction grants to church-related schools in Connecticut. It seems likely that

[1] *Horace Mann League of the United States v. Board of Public Works,* 242 Md. 645, 220 A.2d 51 (1966).

there will be considerably more litigation before the impact of this restriction on grants to church-related institutions is fully delineated.

State constitutional problems are not limited to application of the federal Constitution. More rigid prohibitions against grants of public funds to sectarian schools may be found in 38 state constitutions. In these states, constitutional amendments would have to be adopted before any program of direct state aid to church-related schools could be enacted, even if the grants were within the limitations imposed by the federal Constitution.

Some 900 of all private colleges and universities are church-related. In many states, direct aid to the remaining 500 private independent colleges would also raise constitutional questions. Fourteen states have constitutional provisions explicitly prohibiting appropriations of money or property to privately controlled schools or institutions. Twenty-four states have constitutional provisions prohibiting the state and/or its political subdivisions from appropriating money or property to private individuals or organizations. Thirty-six states have constitutional provisions prohibiting the state and/or its political subdivisions from lending credit to or assuming the liabilities of private individuals or organizations. Twenty-eight states have constitutional provisions prohibiting the state and/or its political subdivisions from becoming joint owners or stockholders in private endeavors. On the other hand, eight states have constitutional provisions specifically authorizing public aid to private schools or for educational purposes under certain conditions.

In the last decade several sectarian colleges have lessened their church connections through a variety of techniques. College management has been separated from the church. Lay members have been appointed to the governing boards. And nonsectarian members have been recruited for the faculty. While many of these moves were undoubtedly undertaken for other policy reasons, an additional impetus for some was the desire to become eligible for public aid.

By making categorical grants, the federal government has provided aid to private institutions without incurring major constitutional obstacles. Both research and construction grants have been made to sectarian colleges on the assumption that the specific purposes of the grants were nonsectarian. There have been some attacks on the constitutionality of these categorical grants, but to date the grants have been upheld.

The most common form of grant which has avoided constitutional barriers is a grant for the benefit of the individual rather than the institution. The student benefit approach has been used for years throughout the educational system without incurring serious constitutional attacks.

New York unsuccessfully attempted to have its constitution amended to permit distribution of its institutional grants to sectarian as well as private independent colleges. The exact limits of New York's ability to make grants to colleges with some church connections have not yet been judicially defined.

It does seem clear, however, that if states were to make grants to private institutions, including sectarian and other church-related institutions, most states would find it necessary to amend their constitutions.

The political feasibility of providing state funds to private institutions may pose greater difficulties than legal problems as such. And since constitutional feasibility may rest on the possibility of obtaining a constitutional amendment, in the long run the constitutional questions also rest on political feasibility. At the present time no state with a major portion of its students in public higher education has established a program of institutional grants to private institutions. Where one has been adopted (New York and, on a somewhat different basis, Pennsylvania), it was possible to demonstrate that without the continuation of private institutions, a much larger expansion would be required in the number of public colleges and universities. But in states where public institutions are carrying the major portion of enrollment in higher education and where there are increasing pressures to slow down the increase in state expenditures on higher education, it is difficult to be convincing when arguing that a program of institutional grants to private institutions from state funds would not simply result in a decrease in funds available for public higher education. It is much more feasible, from a political standpoint, to support particular private institutions for educational services which are clearly needed by the state and which are not available to a sufficient extent from public institutions. Florida's program of aid to private medical schools is an excellent example of this type of program.

For most states, at least in the short-run period, it would seem unlikely that broad programs of general-formula institutional grants for private colleges will be established.

Tuition grants for resident students for use in private institutions could be considered both politically and legally the most feasible way to aid private institutions. But, since tuition at most private institutions covers only a portion of educational costs, tuition grants leading to increased enrollment could actually aggravate the financial pressures unless the institution is operating on an inefficient scale. Even in these circumstances, although unit costs decline, the gap between total expenditures and total revenue may grow. The New York study concluded, after reviewing six years of the state's Scholar Incentive Program, that indirect aid through tuition grants to the student was not adequate for private colleges in New York.

There is no doubt that expanded student aid programs at both the federal and state levels will greatly aid private institutions since it will allow them to shift a portion of the funds which the institution must now provide for financial aid to other purposes. But the financial problems of the private institutions may be greater than this. Several proposals have been made for alleviating these problems, including the Iowa plan for tuition subsidies referred to earlier, a proposal by Howard Bowen, the federal institutional grants bill introduced by Congressman Quie, and the recent proposals in Wisconsin and Illinois. (For brief descriptions of these proposals, see Appendix L.) There are also the several federal aid proposals made by the Carnegie Commission and described elsewhere in this report.

If the financial condition of all or some private institutions in the state indicates need for public support beyond that provided through implementation of the Carnegie Commission recommendations in *Quality and Equality* and the program of tuition grants recommended in the previous chapter, then any resident student selecting such a private institution could be given a cost-of-education voucher which would entitle the institution to a payment from the state.

The amount of this payment should be fixed at some percent of the subsidy granted to public institutions for students at comparable levels. The public institution subsidy can be defined as the difference between instructional costs at a public institution and the required public student fees and tuition. The exact amount of the subsidy in each state would depend upon factors unique to that state, including adequacy of public higher education resources, availability of excess capacity in private higher education, and relative costs of private and public higher education in the state.

The Commission believes that many private institutions are experiencing real financial difficulties. Many of these difficulties could be alleviated by adoption of the Commission's proposals set forth in *Quality and Equality,* as revised in June 1970.

Implementation of these recommendations would:

- Reduce the heavy expenditures of private colleges for student aid through the expanded opportunity grant, work-study, and loan programs
- Help the major private universities through cost-of-education supplements for graduate fellowship recipients and through institutional research grants
- Aid private medical schools through a substantial subsidy for medical students and grants for construction of facilities
- Provide cost-of-education supplements to institutions enrolling undergraduate students eligible for opportunity grants
- Continue aid for private institutional construction at adequate levels, through loans and grants, and interest subsidies on construction loans, with priority given to construction grants to aid institutions to expand to a more efficient size

Two prior recommentations in this report will also be of assistance to private colleges: the recommendation for tuition grants by the states (p. 86), and the recommendation for start-up grants for private institutions (p. 66).

Private institutions also still have some potential for tuition increases. As long as personal disposable income increases, private institutions could increase revenue from this source. More important than this, however, is the potential of both public and private institutions to improve the flow of revenue from donors, alumni, and corporations, particularly; to increase income from endowment funds; and to manage more efficiently those resources it already has.

Many of the state studies on higher education have stressed the great need for both public and private colleges and universities to improve their management practices and to make better utilization of present and potential resources. The North Carolina study stated that "most colleges and universities need to revitalize their operations through more effective allocation of available resources" (14).

The New York study gave evidence of the need for managerial improvement:

Essential management information is lacking in almost every institution studied, and misconceptions concerning the nature and extent of their own financial problems are widespread among top officials in most of the institutions surveyed (7, p. 23).

The Illinois Commission thought this problem important enough to recommend establishing a management advisory service

to assist private institutions in developing systematic long-range planning, institutional research, as well as more effective budgetary procedures, management of business functions, utilization of physical plant, and administration of academic programs . . . (8, p. 56).

The Carnegie Commission recommends that foundations, government agencies, and higher education associations give special attention to funding studies and projects concerned with management problems of universities and colleges with effective utilization of available and potential resources.

It should be noted that efficiency in the use of resources is one of the aspects of higher education that the Carnegie Commission itself has marked out for major research attention.

The Commission also recommends that states enter into agreements, or make grants, for the purpose of continuing certain educational programs at private institutions (for example, Florida and Wisconsin grants to private medical schoools). These should be selected after consideration of special manpower needs, evaluation of existing student places for these programs in public institutions, and the relative costs of expanding public capacity or supporting and expanding private programs.

The Commission also recommends that those states that do not already have programs enabling private institutions to borrow construction funds through a state-created bond-issuing corporation take steps to develop such agencies if the private institutions can demonstrate the need for them.

The Commission believes that the above recommendations along with those already proposed in *Quality and Equality* for federal assistance will, if fully implemented, take care of most of the problems of private institutions in the foreseeable future.

For those few states in which the above recommendations prove inadequate, and this might be the situation in states which rely heavily on private universities and colleges, the Commission recommends that each resident student be given cost-of-education vouchers which would entitle any private institution selected by the student to receive a state payment increasing gradually each year up to an amount equal to one-third of the subsidy granted by the state for students at the same levels attending comparable public institutions.

If states implement this last recommendation, private institutions will find that the grants carry with them demands for greater public accountability and that this may lead to substantial modification of the private institution's concept of institutional independence.

11. Public Accountability and Institutional Independence

A principal concern of many recent state studies of private higher education has been how to provide public support for private institutions without decreasing their institutional independence. The New York Select Committee was charged with the task of finding means to "preserve the strength and vitality of our private and independent institutions of higher education, yet at the same time keep them free." Legislation establishing the Illinois Commission requested advice on how "the nonpublic institutions can be appropriately related to the public ones without impairment of their freedom."

Underlying this concern is the apparently unquestioned assumption that public institutions, because of their public financial support, have substantially less control over their own institutional plans and programs than do prestigious private institutions. Is this linkage between the source of funding and the locus of control as close as the assumption seems to imply? If it is true that publicly supported colleges and universities have demonstrably narrower ranges of independent action, is the potential cost of public support to the private colleges and universities too high?

If private institutions have enhanced American higher education largely because of their relatively greater freedom to experiment, to offer diversity, to control their size, and in general to resist pressures toward homogeneity, will their freedom to continue making contributions of this nature be possible if any significant proportion of their funding comes from public sources? If the control that accompanies public support destroys the freedom which now permits private institutions to make their unique contributions, then the special importance of preserving private higher education may be diminished.

On the other hand, if it is possible to limit effectively the influence or control that may be exercised by the public agency providing funds to a private institution (as the charges to the state committee quoted above seem to imply), it might also be possible to develop guidelines to limit appropriately the areas of influence or control of public agencies over public universities and colleges. In this effort, public and private colleges have a mutual concern and interdependent goals — private colleges want to share in public funds and public colleges want a measure of private autonomy.

PUBLIC FUNDING AND GOVERNMENTAL CONTROL In the early history of the United States, and particularly prior to the Dartmouth Case, colonies and states made grants to private institutions without strings attached. As the distinction between public and private institutions evolved, states ceased giving grants to private institutions and established their own. The degree of control established over state institutions varied among states and also among different types of institutions within the state. In almost all cases, however, the states recognized the need for a greater degree of autonomy for public colleges and universities than that afforded to other agencies of the state.

- Twenty-three states give some form of constitutional recognition to higher education whereas few state departments, other than constitutional offices, are so recognized.

- Forty states confer corporate powers on their highest educational boards (few other departments have them).

- Elections or appointments of board members are for a longer period than for most public offices, and it is often specified that selection of board members be on a nonpolitical basis.

- Many boards have been given direct borrowing power rarely given to state divisions.

- Many are given power to appoint treasurers and select their own depositories and disburse funds, especially institutional funds, directly — a condition very rare in other state agencies.

- Many higher education boards are given wide discretion and in many instances complete autonomy on policy matters, such as admission requirements, graduation requirements, programs, courses, and degrees to be offered.

- Almost all states leave to the higher education boards full authority over all matters relating to academic and professional personnel.

• Most states require more or less complete personnel reporting in connection with the budget but leave final determination to the boards after the appropriation is made. Few boards are given complete authority over administrative and clerical personnel other than the highest administrative position.

Nonetheless, the Committee on Governance and Higher Education, in its report issued in 1959, found substantial encroachments on institutional autonomy. That committee reported that responsibility for purchasing was located in a centralized state agency in 39 states and showed a high degree of centralization in 6 other states. A number of public institutions were subject to pre-audit, and through this pre-audit, state auditors and comptrollers could actually influence educational policy.

In some instances, control of capital expenditures includes centralized development of architectural plans, determination of building priorities, as well as development of space utilization standards.

There are certain states that still include college and university personnel under civil service programs. Rigid rules of such agencies sometimes interfere with the selection of personnel for specialized administrative and clerical positions on a campus, and in those few instances in which they extend to professional and teaching personnel, serious problems result from the centralization of the personnel function.

Through their budget functions, state legislatures have been able to affect the development of new programs, the level of tuition charges, and the establishment of new campuses.

In the last decade, the establishment of coordinating and planning agencies has led to the danger of further erosion of institutional independence of public colleges and universities. If the regulatory powers of these agencies are limited to powers which were formerly lodged in the legislature, presumably there is simply a different locus of external power rather than an erosion of the previous level of institutional independence. But even in these instances, a more active exercise of these external controls may lead to some erosion of institutional independence. Conversely, strong coordinating agencies concerned with preservation of institutional independence could protect institutions from legislative encroachments on their independence.

Although variations in the degree of state control do exist, there is no question that state-supported institutions do not enjoy the same degree of institutional independence as many private institutions. This is not to say that private institutions are free from external control but, rather, that they are not subject to the type of centralized state control which in some states threatens the independence of public institutions.

EXPERIENCE WITH PUBLIC GRANTS TO PRIVATE INSTITUTIONS As mentioned earlier in the report, there is relatively little experience in this country with general programs of state aid to private institutions. Pennsylvania, which has had a program of aid to selected private institutions for many years, does exercise a greater degree of control over those private institutions that receive aid than over other private institutions. The degree to which institutional independence will be affected by the general institutional aid program in New York is not yet known. Early reports indicate that private institutions in that state receiving institutional grants must supply to the state a great deal of information that formerly had not been required.

Federal grants have been available to private as well as public institutions for several years. Up to this time these grants have usually carried with them influence but have stopped short of actual control. The research grants certainly influence the development of particular educational programs within institutions receiving those grants. Availability of construction grants has had definite impacts on institutional policy decisions. Availability of support funds for various categories of graduate students and the cost of education allowances which accompanied these funds have influenced the growth of various graduate departments.

Several reasons have been suggested for the lesser degree of control accompanying federal grants than those accompanying state grants. Federal grants have been made to almost a thousand institutions in the 50 states. Control involving this number of units is much more difficult than control by a state when its grants are given to a few public higher education segments or to a few private institutions.

The federal government does not have the same sense of identification with the institution as does the state. Federal grants are usually made for specific purposes rather than for general educational expenses of the institution.

Nonetheless, when there has been an overriding national goal involving higher education, the federal government has attached requirements to these limited purpose grants to influence all aspects of institutional activity toward achievement of such a goal. Its interest in eliminating discrimination on the basis of race, creed, color, or national origin led the federal government to impose controls designed to achieve this national interest on all institutions, whether public or private, receiving federal aid without regard to the particular purpose of the aid.

In Great Britain, when it became essential to provide public funds for independent institutions, the University Grants Committee (UGC) was established to allocate such funds. In its early period the UGC served as an effective buffer between the government and the institutions. It was characterized as an indication of the government's willingness to provide money for the universities "without strings." The UGC does, however, set certain standards for use of the funds. All building plans require UGC approval that they are consistent with norms established by the Committee and all salary scales are set by the Committee. Recently the UGC has been shifted from the Treasury to the Ministry of Education and Science and requirements have been introduced to open university books to the Comptroller and Auditor-General.

As the visibility of the grant increases in the total budget of the granting agency, there are strong indications that the degree of control by that agency also increases. Thus, as appropriations for higher education became larger in England, a somewhat closer watch was kept on expenditures. And in those states in which appropriations for higher education are beginning to constitute significant proportions of the general fund expenditures, state offices are becoming more regulatory in their approach to state university and college operations. There is a vast difference in the general posture of a granting agency, such as the federal government, whose higher education expenditures constitute only about 3 percent of its total budget and a granting agency, such as many states today, in which higher education appropriations constitute much larger proportions of the general fund expenditures.

A further push toward greater control may result from the growing public involvement in higher education. That involvement has risen both through expanded enrollment and through activities on campuses which attract news media attention. The recent campus unrest has led to introduction of numerous bills, in both the federal and state legislative bodies, which could seriously infringe upon efforts of institutions to govern themselves.

PUBLIC ACCOUNTABILITY Under no circumstances can institutional independence be considered absolute. Not even its strongest advocates can seriously question the legitimacy of requiring some degree of public accountability from educational institutions receiving public support. Indeed, it can be argued that all educational institutions, whether or not they receive direct public support, incur some measure of public responsibility. All are answerable to the general laws which affect them, and, since all educational institutions receive some special tax privileges, they incur certain public responsibilities. Furthermore, all institutions have a responsibility to their own constituents and to their immediate environs to operate the institutions in a reasonably orderly fashion; they also have a responsibility, particularly to their students, to provide the type of education for which the students contracted. But the broader types of public accountability involving general fiscal controls, responsibility for manpower development, and responsibility for meeting general societal education demands are usually limited to those institutions which obtain a significant portion of their funds from public sources.

The techniques used to achieve public accountability of educational institutions must be balanced against the need of educational institutions for that degree of institutional independence which is essential for their continued vitality.

THE CASE FOR INSTITUTIONAL INDEPENDENCE Among the most significant reasons for preserving institutional independence are the following:

- A viable society requires institutions of higher education with sufficient independence so that their numbers feel free to comment upon, criticize, and advise on a great variety of policies and practices.

- Creative research and effective teaching require freedom. Great strides in higher education have been made by those institutions that were relatively free from external governmental control.

- Freedom from external control facilitates intelligent planning.

- External control often inhibits the type of experimentation and innovation required for continued improvement of our educational resources.

- Efficient operation requires that degree of institutional independence needed for intelligent management.

- Also, in a country, such as France, with a single national system of higher education, every important university and college issue becomes a potential political issue. Our pluralistic system has helped to prevent this, to the advantage of both the colleges and universities, and the body politic.

Our pluralistic structure for higher education has given us a system with strength and vitality unparalleled in any other nation.

GUIDELINES FOR INSTITUTIONAL INDEPENDENCE To state the case for institutional independence does little to preserve it. To achieve freedom for university faculties it was necessary to define in relatively concrete terms the essential elements of academic freedom. While there may continue to be disagreements on the exact meaning of academic freedom, there is some general agreement about the central elements of the concept. But institutional independence or autonomy is yet to be defined. The two concepts are not entirely independent of one another. Indeed, a degree of institutional independence may be essential to preserve academic freedom.

For institutions which are largely supported by the state, the Commission believes that the following are matters over which it seems appropriate for the state to exercise influence and even control:

1 Numbers of places available in state institutions as a total and in specific programs where there are clear manpower needs (e.g., medicine)

2 Number and location of new campuses

3 Minimum and maximum size of institutions by type

4 General admissions policy (i.e., whether open door or selective)

5 General level of institutional budgets, including construction budgets

6 General level of salaries

7 Accounting practices

8 General functions of institutions

9 Major new endeavors

10 Effective use of resources

11 Continued effective operation of the institutions within the general law

State control of the above matters must, of course, stop short of interference with the governance of the institution within broadly established policies. The Commission believes that the following limitations must be placed on state involvement in order to permit the institution that freedom of judgment on institutional operation necessary for effective management:

- External budget control should be limited to the total amount of the budget and to post-audit for purposes of determining fiscal responsibility and should not involve line-item approval, involvement in budget management, or specific allocation of resources within the institution.

- Salary scales for individual classifications should not be set by external authority, nor should mix of faculty or staff at various levels be determined by external authority.

- General levels of admission may be determined externally, but external authorities should not be involved in the development of a policy to meet those levels or in the application of admission policies to individual cases.

- The hiring, firing, and assignment of faculty and staff should be within the internal control of the institution.

- While space utilization standards and maximum costs per square foot are legitimately a matter of external policy, building and equipment design should not be.

Beyond these limitations, universities and colleges must be assured the essential elements of academic freedom if they are to exist and function as educational institutions. These elements are:

- The appointment and promotion of faculty members and of administrators

- Determination of courses of instruction and content of courses

- Selection of individual students

- Awarding of individual degrees

- Selection and conduct of individual research projects, and freedom to publish and otherwise disseminate research results

- Freedom of inquiry

- Freedom of speech, assembly, and other constitutional freedoms so central to the educational process

GUARDING
THE GUIDE-
LINES

Defense of academic freedom in this country has been enhanced by the vigilant surveillance of the American Association of University Professors and its censures of institutions that infringe upon academic freedom. An appropriate agency would also be helpful to guard against infringement on institutional independence. It is difficult to suggest an agency in a sufficiently independent position to feel free to censure the state. However, it is possible to reduce the potential for encroachments upon institutional independence by assuring a composition of public institution governing boards and state coordinating councils that militate against too great and too early an involvement of the state in key educational policy matters and in the administration of the institution. Certainly one major step in this direction would be the reduction of the number of state officers who serve as ex officio members of governing boards and the establishment of a system to screen and/or confirm appointments to boards.

The Commission recommends that:

1 Public and private institutions seek to establish guidelines clearly defining the limitations on state concern and state regulation or control

2 A special commission on institutional independence be established within the American Council on Education; this commission, which should consist of both ACE members and public members, would be assigned responsibility for reviewing external interference with institutional independence and issuing findings after such reviews

3 Elected officials (unless elected for that specific purpose) not serve as members of governing boards of public institutions or coordinating agencies

4 A system be developed to assure adequate screening and consultation prior to appointments to governing boards, regardless of who has the final authority to appoint

For private institutions receiving some public support, the appropriate matters for state concern would depend on the type of grant. In limited purpose or categorical grants, it is certainly appropriate for the granting agency to take steps to assure that the funds are spent for the purposes intended. As private institutions receive general institutional grants from the state, areas of appropriate state concern could more closely resemble those for state institutions. It would be well for private institutions to aid public institutions in establishing the guidelines mentioned above and in gaining adherence to them. Otherwise the cost of state general institutional grants to private institutions might be much too high for both the private institutions and society.

There are other conditions that are conducive to reducing external control of colleges and universities. Diversity of funding, including obtaining some revenue from individuals (both students and alumni), militates against concentrations of assumed power. Resistance to adding layers to the external decision-making processes by relying on state planning and coordinating agencies, rather than on super-boards with administrative responsibilities, helps to avoid unnecessary infringements on institutional independence.

It is also possible that establishment of boards for each campus within a multicampus institution would be advantageous. With a single board for many campuses, an event on any one campus affects the whole system. Also, it is easier for political authorities to sit on and to control a single board than it is for them to do so on multiple boards. Furthermore, a board for each campus would tend to result in a board more responsive to the needs of the particular campus — the members of the board would become more familiar with the faculty, students, and administrators as well as the programs at the institution and, presumably, could identify more closely with the institution and therefore be in a better position to act as a buffer in times of adverse public reaction. On the other hand, in certain communities, a local board with members who are drawn from the community of the institution might act as a more effective conduit of any adverse public reaction. It is also possible that a board more intimately connected with the institution might be tempted more frequently to involve itself in administrative matters. On balance, however, the advantages for the establishment of a board for each campus, particularly if the campuses are large and if there is some differentiation in educational programs and characteristics of the campuses, would seem to be a better course than the establishment of a governing board with several major campuses under its jurisdiction.

Institutional freedom is more easily fostered if each institution has its own personnel system, at least for faculty members, rather than including university personnel in the civil service system as in Germany or France; if students are given free choice of institutions and programs rather than being officially directed into programs; and if the pluralistic system is maintained as opposed to a single system such as that in France.

And perhaps most important, pressure for state interference is considerably less intense when institutions conduct themselves within the law, provide a high level of performance, maintain institutional neutrality in electoral politics, and develop constructive and communicative contacts with the public.

12. Conclusion

In the decade of the 1960s, higher education experienced what might, in retrospect, be called a golden era. The pressures of rapidly rising demands for higher education placed a great strain on institutions, but states seemed willing and able to provide the necessary leadership and funding to greatly increase the capacity of public institutions so that all qualified students could be accommodated. During the last decade state and local funds for higher education quadrupled. It was only through this massive state effort that the nation was able to move somewhat closer to the goal of equal educational opportunity. The decades of the 1970s may prove to be a severe contrast with the sixties. Signs of financial stringency are already manifest in many states, and in many colleges and universities. Public institutions are torn between the desire to achieve true open access at the very moment that a shortage of funds suggests the need to curtail enrollment. CUNY (City University of New York) with its dramatic open-access experiment is an excellent example of an institution in this dilemma. Private institutions, which seemed to get along without state aid in the 1960s, are now insisting that they too must have public funds. And increasing campus unrest makes heavily burdened taxpayers less willing to support expanded appropriations for higher education.

Nonetheless, if American higher education is to survive the seventies and still retain its present quality, states must make a further vigorous effort to provide their fair share of the resources needed to accommodate the 3 million enrollment increase expected in the seventies. What is the state's fair share, and what kind of financial and other efforts should be expected from states in the 1970s?

One measure of whether a state is carrying its share of the na-

	State	Ratio
TABLE 9 **Number of** **undergraduates** **enrolled in** **state per 100** **eighteen-to** **twenty-one-year-** **olds in state** **(1968)**	District of Columbia	102
	Utah	83
	Massachusetts	68
	Colorado	61
	Vermont	61
	Oregon	61
	Arizona	61
	New York	59
	California	58
	Nebraska	58
	Wisconsin	57
	Oklahoma	56
	South Dakota	56
	Kansas	55
	Iowa	55
	Wyoming	54
	Washington	54
	Rhode Island	53
	Minnesota	52
	Idaho	52
	Missouri	52
	Connecticut	51
	Michigan	50
	Indiana	50
	North Dakota	50
	Illinois	50
	New Hampshire	49
	Montana	47
	Pennsylvania	46
	Ohio	45
	New Mexico	44
	West Virginia	44
	Texas	43
	Tennessee	42
	Louisiana	42
	Florida	42

State	Ratio
Kentucky	39
Maryland	38
Mississippi	37
Hawaii	36
Arkansas	36
Alabama	36
Delaware	35
New Jersey	33
North Carolina	32
Maine	31
Georgia	29
Virginia	27
Nevada	26
South Carolina	22
Alaska	10
TOTAL U.S.	48

tional burden of providing places for students is the state's ratio of total public and private student places to the number of 18- to 21-year-olds in the state. The range among states on this ratio is very great: the District of Columbia actually has more than 100 places for every 100 in the age group; Alaska, just beginning to build its higher education system, has only 10 places per 100 in the age group (see Table 9). We believe that states whose ratio is less than 30 to 100 are clearly not carrying their fair share of the national higher education effort.

The Commission recommends that states having a ratio of less than 30 places in both public and private higher education in the state for every 100 eighteen- to twenty-one-year-olds in the state should take emergency measures to increase the availability of higher education in the state.

Currently, states are providing 28 percent of college and university income. The Carnegie Commission has recommended in its report *Quality and Equality* that federal funds for higher education be increased and that there be a relative decline in the state's share. The Commission believes that this relative decline will be very small over the next ten years. It would certainly seem that states will have to continue to supply approximately one-quarter of the total funding required for colleges and universities.

In 1966–67 approximately 0.7 percent of per capita personal income was spent through state and local taxes for higher education. To accommodate the expanded enrollment expected in the next decade, the amount spent on higher education through state and local taxes will have to increase to approximately 1 percent of personal per capita income taking into account the slight relative decline expected in the state's share of financing higher education. Without this slight decline in the state share, it would be necessary to increase this figure to 1.2 percent of per capita personal income. The Commission believes that states far below this level at the present time should make an emergency effort to increase their financial support of higher education.

The Commission recommends that states with a present expenditure of less than 0.6 percent of per capita personal income spent through state and local taxes for higher education should take immediate steps to increase their financial support of higher education.

Using 1966–67 expenditure figures, under this recommendation it would be necessary for Maine, Delaware, Virginia, New Hampshire, Pennsylvania, Connecticut, Ohio, Massachusetts, and New Jersey to increase their financial support for higher education.

The Commission also believes that states can maximize the benefit of their expenditures on higher education and strengthen the colleges and universities in their states by participating in the regional cooperative activities undertaken through the regional boards (Western Interstate Commission on Higher Education, Southern Regional Education Board, and New England Board of Higher Education). Still very young organizations, these agencies have shown great potential for aiding the states in the improvement of their higher educational systems. On the national scale, the Education Commission of the States also makes this possible.

The tests mentioned above (expenditures on higher education and the availability of higher education places with particular reference to 18- to 21-year-olds) are especially relevant for the immediate future. However, the long-range test of a state's system can be met only if the state has also broadened its concern to include the entire range of postsecondary education and has educational opportunities available to meet the various educational needs and qualifications of its citizens throughout their lives and to develop the leadership, professional, and technical skills needed by the society.

References

1 Willingham, Warren W.: "Free-Access Colleges: Where and When They Serve," *College Board Review,* vol. 76, pp. 6–14, Summer 1970.

2 Post High School Study Committee: *Education Beyond the High School: A Projection for Oregon,* 1966, p. 275.

3 Froomkin, Joseph: *Aspirations, Enrollments, and Resources,* U.S. Office of Education, Washington, D.C., 1970, p. 42.

4 Bowen, William G.: *The Economics of the Major Private Universities,* Carnegie Commission on Higher Education, Berkeley, Calif., 1968, pp. 53–56.

5 Pfnister, Allan O., and Gary Quehl: *Report on the Status of Private Higher Education in the State of Missouri,* Springfield, Ohio, 1967, part II, p. 17.

6 Liaison Committee on Texas Private Colleges and Universities: *Pluralism and Partnership,* Austin, 1968, p. 41.

7 New York Select Committee on the Future of Private and Independent Higher Education in New York State: *New York State and Private Higher Education,* State Education Department, Albany, 1968, p. 15.

8 Commission to Study Non-Public Higher Education in Illinois: *Strengthening Private Higher Education in Illinois,* Springfield, 1969, p. 23.

9 Select Committee for the Study of Financial Problems of Private Institutions of Higher Education in the Commonwealth of Massachusetts: *Financial Problems of Massachusetts Private Higher Education,* 1970, p. 3.

10 Independent Colleges and Universities of Indiana: *Strengthening Independent Higher Education in the State of Indiana,* Indianapolis, 1970, pp. 16, 25.

11 Cheit, Earl F.: *The New Depression in Higher Education,* McGraw-Hill Book Company, New York, 1971.

12 Cary, William L., and Craig B. Bright: *The Law and the Lore of Endowment Funds,* Ford Foundation, 1969.

13 U.S. Bureau of Labor Statistics: *Three Budgets for an Urban Family of Four Persons: Preliminary Spring 1969 Cost Estimates,* Washington, D.C., 1969, table 1.

14 North Carolina Board of Higher Education: *Planning for Higher Education in North Carolina,* Raleigh, N.C., 1968.

Appendix A:
Percent of College and University Students Enrolled in Private Institutions (1968)

State	Percent
Alabama	19
Alaska	12
Arizona	2
Arkansas	23
California	13
Colorado	15
Connecticut	49
Delaware	13
District of Columbia	92
Florida	24
Georgia	22
Hawaii	10
Idaho	25
Illinois	37
Indiana	31
Iowa	42
Kansas	17
Kentucky	25
Louisiana	17
Maine	32
Maryland	27
Massachusetts	69

State	Percent
Michigan	16
Minnesota	20
Mississippi	13
Missouri	30
Montana	11
Nebraska	26
Nevada	0
New Hampshire	49
New Jersey	41
New Mexico	9
New York	47
North Carolina	36
North Dakota	4
Ohio	29
Oklahoma	19
Oregon	15
Pennsylvania	48
Rhode Island	53
South Carolina	37
South Dakota	24
Tennessee	32
Texas	20
Utah	37
Vermont	53
Virginia	24
Washington	16
West Virginia	21
Wisconsin	20
Wyoming	0

SOURCE: Enrollment data from National Center for Educational Statistics, *Opening Fall Enrollment,* 1968. Enrollments include degree-credit enrollment (both extension and resident) at all institutions listed in the U.S. Office of Education Directory of Institutions of Higher Education.

Appendix B: Characteristics of State Coordinating Mechanisms

PART A *Composition and scope of agency, as of March 1, 1971*

State	Name of agency	How established	Date established	K–12	2-yr. coll.
Alabama	Higher Education Commission	Statute	1969	–	x
Alaska	Board of Regents	Constitution and statute	1935	–	–
Arizona	Board of Regents	Statute	1945	–	–
Arkansas	Commission on Coordination of Higher Education Finance	Statute	1961	–	x
California	Coordinating Council for Higher Education	Statute	1960	–	x
Colorado	Commission on Higher Education	Statute	1965	–	x
Connecticut	Commission for Higher Education	Statute	1965	–	x
Florida	Board of Regents	Statute	1905	–	–
Georgia	Board of Regents	Constitution and statute	1931	–	x
Hawaii	Board of Regents	Statute	1920	–	–
Idaho	State Board of Education	Statute	1912	x	x
Illinois	Board of Higher Education	Statute	1957	–	x
Iowa	State Board of Regents	Statute	1909	–	–
Kansas	Board of Regents	Constitution and statute	1913	–	–
Kentucky	Council on Public Higher Education	Statute	1934	–	x
Louisiana	Coordinating Council for Higher Education	Statute	1969	–	x
Maine	Board of Trustees of University of Maine	Statute	1968	–	–
Maryland	Maryland Council for Higher Education	Statute	1964	–	x
Massachusetts	Board of Higher Education	Statute	1965	–	x
Michigan	State Board of Education	Constitution and statute	1963	x	x
Minnesota	Higher Education Coordinating Commission	Statute	1965	–	x
Mississippi	Board of Trustees of State Institutions of Higher Learning	Statute	1910	–	–
Missouri	Commission on Higher Education	Statute	1963	–	x

General scope		Composition of board[2]						
4-yr. coll. & univ.	*Private coll. & univ.*[1]	*No. on board*	*Appt. by gov.*	*Elected*	*State officials*	*Public inst.*	*Private inst.*	*Term of appointment (years)*[3]
x	–	9	9	–	–	–	–	9
x	–	8	8	–	–	–	–	8
x	–	10	8	–	2	–	–	8
x	–	10	10	–	–	–	–	10
x	–	10	7	–	–	3	1[6]	4
x	–	9	9	–	–	–	–	4
x	x	16	12	–	–	4[4]	–	8
x	–	9	9	–	–	–	–	9
x	–	15	15	–	–	–	–	7
x	–	9	9	–	–	–	–	
x	–	9	7	–	2	–	–	5
x	–	16	10	–	1	5	–	6
x	–	9	9	–	–	–	–	6
x	–	9	9	–	–	–	–	4
x	–	17	9	–	–	8[5]	–	4
x	–	15	13	–	–	2[4]	–	6
x	–	15	15	–	–	–	–	
x	–	13	9	–	–	3	1[6]	6[3]
x	–	11	6	–	–	4	1[6]	5
x	–	10	–	8	2[7]	–	–	8
x	–[17]	18	8	–	–	8[8]	2[8]	4
x	–	13	12,	–	–	1[9]	–	12
x	–	10	6	–	–	3[10]	1[10]	6

State	Name of agency	How established	Date established	K–12	2-yr. coll.
Montana	State Board of Education	Statute	1889	x	–
Nebraska	Coordinating Council Steering Committee	Voluntary	1966	–	x
Nevada	Board of Regents	Constitution and statute	1864	–	–
New Hampshire	Board of Trustees	Statute	1963	–	–
New Jersey	Board of Higher Education	Statute	1967	–	x
New Mexico	Board of Educational Finance	Statute	1951	–	x
New York	Board of Regents	Statute	1784	x	x
North Carolina	Board of Higher Education	Statute	1955	–	–
North Dakota	State Board of Higher Education	Statute	1911	–	x
Ohio	Board of Regents	Statute	1963	–	x
Oklahoma	State Regents for Higher Education	Constitution and statute	1941	–	x
Oregon	State Board of Higher Education	Statute	1929	–	–
Pennsylvania	State Board of Education	Statute	1963	x	x
Rhode Island	Board of Regents for Higher Education	Statute	1969	x	x
South Carolina	State Commission on Higher Education	Statute	1967	–	x
South Dakota	Board of Regents	Statute	1897	–	–
Tennessee	Higher Education Commission	Statute	1967	–	x
Texas	Coordinating Board, Texas University & College System	Statute	1965	–	x
Utah	State Board of Higher Education	Statute	1969	–	x
Virginia	State Council of Higher Education	Statute	1956	–	–
Washington	Council on Higher Education	Statute	1969	–	x
West Virginia	Board of Regents	Statute	1969	–	–
Wisconsin	Coordinating Council for Higher Education	Statute	1955	–	x
Wyoming	Higher Education Council	Statute	1969	–	x

General scope		Composition of board[2]						Term of
4-yr. coll. & univ.	*Private coll. & univ.*[1]	*No. on board*	*Appt. by gov.*	*Elected*	*State officials*	*Public inst.*	*Private inst.*	*appointment (years)*[3]
x	–	11	8	–	3	–	–	8
x	–	–	–	–	–	10	–	–
x	–	9	–	9	–	–	–	4
x	–	24	12	–	3	9[11]	–	4
x	x	18	9	–	2[5]	6	1[12]	6
x	–	11	11	–	–	–	–	6
x	x	15	–	By legislature	–	–	–	15
x	–	22	9	–	7[13]	6	–	6
x	–	7	7	–	–	–	–	7
x	–	11	9	–	2[5]	–	–	9
x	x	9	9	–	–	–	–	9
x	–	9	9	–	–	–	–	6
x	–	17	17	–	–	–	–	6
x	–	9	9	–	–	–	–	4
x	–	14	7	–	–	7	–	4
x	–	7	7	–	–	–	–	6
x	–	9	9	–	–	–	–	9
x	–	18	18	–	–	–	–	6
x	–	15	15	–	–	–	–	6
x	–	11	11	–	–	–	–	4
x	–	25	9	–	6[14]	8[5]	2[15]	6
x	–	10	9	–	1[5]	–	–	6
x	–	17	10[16]	–	1	6	–	8
x	–	7	3	–	1	3	–	5

[1] The agency is noted as having private universities and colleges within its scope only if it appears from the statute that the agency has responsibilities with respect to private institutions similar to those for public institutions.

[2] Unless otherwise noted, institutional representatives are appointed by the trustees of the institution or serve because of their position as chairman of trustees or president of the institution. The state officials may include the governor, members of the legislature, and superintendent of public instruction.

[3] The term of appointment shown is usually only applicable to the appointed public members.

[4] Includes member of State Board of Education.

[5] Nonvoting members.

[6] Governor must appoint one person for private colleges.

[7] The ex-officio members are without votes.

[8] Governor must appoint two members who are presidents of two private colleges or universities in the state and eight who are trustees or chief executive officers of the four public institutions.

[9] Governor appoints one trustee for Lebauve fund (Lebauve family made a large gift to the University of Mississippi). The Lebauve trustee has the right to vote only on matters affecting the University of Mississippi.

[10] Governor is requested to appoint one junior college president, one state college president, one private institution president, and the chief administrator of the University of Missouri.

[11] Six of the institutional representatives are elected by the alumni of the three state institutions.

[12] The private college representative is designated by the Association of Independent Colleges and Universities of New Jersey.

[13] Includes governors, chairmen of state house and senate committees on finance, appropriations, and higher education.

[14] Includes four legislators appointed by the Speaker of the House and the president of the Senate and two members of the Governor's staff appointed by him to serve at his pleasure. These six members serve on the council but do not have the right to vote.

[15] The Governor is required to appoint two presidents of private institutions. These serve without vote.

[16] Includes one member of County Teachers College Board whom the governor is required to appoint annually.

[17] Some statutory responsibilities for private institutions but not as extensive as those for public institutions.

NOTE: Delaware and Indiana have no coordinating agency or consolidated governing board and thus are not included in the above table.

PART B   *Functions of agency[1], as of March 1, 1971*

State	Institutional budget responsibilities: state funds				Receipt and allocation of HEFA funds
	Review and advise	Prepare consolidated budget	Approve	Allocate	
Alabama	x	x	–	–	–
Arkansas	x	x	–	–	x
California	x	–	–	–	x
Colorado	x[8]	–	–	–	x
Connecticut	x	–	–	–	–
Illinois	x	–	–	–	x
Kentucky	x	–	–	–	–
Louisiana	x	–	–	–	–
Maryland	x	–	–	–	–
Massachusetts	x	–	–	–	x
Michigan	x	–	–	–	x
Minnesota	x[12]	–	–	–	x
Missouri	x	–	–	–	x

Capital outlays	New campuses[3]	New degrees	New programs	Degree requirements	Enrollment limits	Admission requirements[4]	Accreditation	Long-range planning (explicit references in statutes)
								—approval authority[2] a—advisory responsibility[2]
–	–	a	a	–	–	–	–	To recommend legislation . . . for orderly growth and overall development of . . . public higher education.
a	a	–	–	–	–	–	–	Conducts continuing studies in all matters involving finances and capital improvements.
a	a	a[5]	a	–	–	a	–	Develop plans for orderly growth of public higher education.
*	a	*	*	–	a	a	–	Make studies toward further development of state policy in higher education and maintain a comprehensive plan.
a	*	*	*	–	a	–	*[6]	Be responsible for coordination of planning for higher education throughout the state.
*	*	*	*	–	*	*	–	Prepare a master plan for the development, expansion, integration, coordination and efficient use of facilities, curriculum, and standards of public higher education.
–	a[7]	–	–	–	–	*	–	Develop comprehensive plans for public higher education.
a	*	*	*	–	–	–	–	Prepare a master plan for coordination, development, and organization of public higher education.
a	a	–	a	–	a	–	–	Preparation of programs for the orderly growth and overall development of the . . . public higher education.
a	a	*[6]	*	–	–	–	–	Plan and support orderly and feasible expansion of each segment of public higher education, as a whole.
–	*	*	*	–	–	–	–	General planning and coordinating body for all public education including higher education.
a	a	a	a	–	–	–	–	Continuously engage in long-range planning.
a	a	a	a	–	a	a	–	Responsibility for designing a coordinated plan for higher education.

State	Institutional budget responsibilities: state funds				Receipt and allocation of HEFA funds
	Review and advise	*Prepare consolidated budget*	*Approve*	*Allocate*	
New Jersey	x	x	–	–	x
New Mexico	–	–	x	–	x
New York	–	–	–	–	x
North Carolina	x	–	–	–	–
Ohio	x	–	–	–	–[10]
Oklahoma	–	x	–	x	x
Pennsylvania	x	–	–	–	–
South Carolina	x	–	–	–	–
Tennessee	x	–	–	–	–
Texas	x	–	–	–	–
Virginia	x	–	–	–	–
Washington	x	–	–	–	x
Wisconsin	x	x	–	–	–
Wyoming	x	–	–	–	x

Capital outlays	New campuses[3]	New degrees	New programs	Degree requirements	Enrollment limits	Admission requirements[4]	Accreditation	Long-range planning (explicit references in statutes)
								—approval authority[2] a—advisory responsibility[2]
*	*	*	*	*	*	*	*	Develop and maintain a comprehensive master plan which shall be long-run in nature and be regularly revised and updated.
*	–	–	–	–	–	–	–	No explicit provision.
–	–	*	*	*	–	–	*[6]	Submit to legislature plan for expansion and development of higher education.
a	*	*[5]	*[5]	a	–	–	–[11]	Plan and coordinate the major educational functions and activities of higher education in the state.
a	*[9]	*	*	–	–	–	–	Formulate a master plan for higher education.
*	*	*	*	*		*	*	No explicit provision.
a	–	–	–	a	–	–	–	Develop a master plan
a	a	*	*	a	a	a	a	Study . . . the role of state-supported higher education in serving the needs of the state.
a	*	*	*	–	–	–	–	To develop a master plan for future development of higher education.
*	a	*	*	–	–	a	–	No explicit provision.
a	a	*	*	–	–	–	–	Develop plans under which the several state-supported institutions of higher education in Virginia shall constitute a coordinated system.
a	a	a	a	–	a	–	–	Engage in overall planning for higher education in state.
a	a	*	*	–	–	–	–	Adopt a coordinating plan for the integration and most efficient use of the existing facilities and personnel, and an order of priority for construction of facilities.
a	a	–	–	–	–	–	–	Develop plans for the orderly growth of higher education and location of new facilities and programs.

[1] Not included in this part are those states without any coordination mechanism or those states with consolidated governing boards. The consolidated governing board tends to exercise the usual management responsibilities.

The functions listed are, for the most part, those explicitly stated in the legislation, except that additional interpretations of functions were obtained directly from the agencies.

[2] Unless noted otherwise the authority indicated here relates only to public institutions.

[3] *New campuses* is interpreted to include new institutions.

[4] Where an agency sets admission standards, they are usually minimum standards — in some instances explicitly permitting the institution to be more selective.

[5] Does not include community colleges.

[6] Includes private institutions.

[7] Has approval authority for professional schools but recommends on others.

[8] Reviews and revises institutional requests and submits revised recommendations to the legislature.

[9] Only for two-year colleges.

[10] Advises on allocation of these funds.

[11] Both public and private institutions must be licensed by agency to grant degrees.

[12] Review on a selective basis and establishment of certain budgeting standards and guidelines.

Appendix C: Ratio of Residents of State Enrolled as Undergraduates in Any State to Number of 18- to 21- Year- Olds in State (1968)

State	Student residents	Number of 18- to 21-year-olds	Ratio
Alabama	80,648	254,700	.32
Alaska	4,207	29,200	.14
Arizona	59,898	125,300	.48
Arkansas	44,682	133,000	.34
California	704,728	1,413,500	.50
Colorado	64,229	150,900	.43
Connecticut	97,416	189,800	.51
Delaware	11,709	38,100	.31
District of Columbia	17,937	59,900	.30
Florida	160,444	424,800	.38
Georgia	86,835	352,900	.25
Hawaii	22,068	68,100	.32
Idaho	25,089	48,900	.51
Illinois	332,353	701,800	.47
Indiana	121,682	341,600	.36
Iowa	81,036	178,000	.46
Kansas	74,218	164,500	.45
Kentucky	71,834	229,600	.31
Louisiana	94,331	268,600	.35
Maine	18,421	70,400	.26

State	Student residents	Number of 18- to 21-year-olds	Ratio
Maryland	99,404	275,600	.36
Massachusetts	170,968	352,500	.49
Michigan	236,564	583,900	.41
Minnesota	108,397	240,400	.45
Mississippi	56,435	170,600	.33
Missouri	120,211	298,000	.40
Montana	23,362	51,800	.45
Nebraska	46,025	102,900	.45
Nevada	9,461	35,600	.27
New Hampshire	16,322	46,700	.35
New Jersey	207,584	449,400	.46
New Mexico	31,843	82,600	.39
New York	600,626	1,161,300	.52
North Carolina	90,529	385,200	.24
North Dakota	22,815	47,900	.48
Ohio	271,004	713,100	.38
Oklahoma	79,095	171,500	.46
Oregon	66,459	138,300	.48
Pennsylvania	294,698	731,300	.40
Rhode Island	24,704	63,800	.39
South Carolina	41,993	210,900	.20
South Dakota	22,765	48,100	.47
Tennessee	86,045	277,800	.31
Texas	302,136	814,800	.37
Utah	41,103	77,800	.53
Vermont	9,384	27,700	.34
Virginia	97,698	371,100	.26
Washington	107,227	231,100	.46
West Virginia	39,615	121,400	.33
Wisconsin	122,230	275,200	.44
Wyoming	11,799	22,800	.52
50 states and Washington, D.C.	5,632,266	13,809,000	.41

SOURCE: U.S. Office of Education unpublished data on residence and migration of college students, fall 1968. Estimates derived by the Carnegie Commission staff using Bureau of the Census *Current Population Reports,* Ser. P-25, nos. 375 and 416, and 1960 census data for the states.

Appendix D: Ratio of Resident Undergraduate Students Enrolled in State of Residence to Number of 18- to 21- Year-Olds in State (1968)

State	Students remaining	Number of 18- to 21-year-olds	Ratio
Alabama	71,750	254,700	.28
Alaska	2,206	29,200	.08
Arizona	54,069	125,300	.43
Arkansas	38,847	133,000	.29
California	669,323	1,413,500	.47
Colorado	55,564	150,900	.37
Connecticut	60,562	189,800	.32
Delaware	6,780	38,100	.18
District of Columbia	9,969	59,900	.17
Florida	134,269	424,800	.32
Georgia	73,069	352,900	.21
Hawaii	15,392	68,100	.23
Idaho	19,078	48,900	.39
Illinois	263,425	701,800	.38
Indiana	104,520	341,600	.31
Iowa	62,514	178,000	.35
Kansas	65,147	164,500	.40
Kentucky	62,032	229,600	.27
Louisiana	87,815	268,600	.33

State	Students remaining	Number of 18- to 21-year-olds	Ratio
Maine	12,822	70,400	.18
Maryland	73,725	275,600	.27
Massachusetts	135,648	352,500	.38
Michigan	220,585	583,900	.38
Minnesota	94,239	240,400	.39
Mississippi	51,413	170,600	.30
Missouri	102,650	298,000	.34
Montana	19,438	51,800	.38
Nebraska	39,974	102,900	.39
Nevada	6,728	35,600	.19
New Hampshire	10,231	46,700	.22
New Jersey	109,314	449,400	.24
New Mexico	26,545	82,600	.32
New York	489,295	1,161,300	.42
North Carolina	81,041	385,200	.21
North Dakota	19,169	47,900	.40
Ohio	229,423	713,100	.32
Oklahoma	72,486	171,500	.42
Oregon	58,860	138,300	.43
Pennsylvania	231,100	731,300	.32
Rhode Island	17,847	63,800	.28
South Carolina	32,503	210,900	.15
South Dakota	19,504	48,100	.41
Tennessee	75,641	277,800	.27
Texas	285,976	814,800	.35
Utah	39,413	77,800	.51
Vermont	6,252	27,700	.23
Virginia	66,964	371,100	.18
Washington	97,663	231,100	.42
West Virginia	34,593	121,400	.28
Wisconsin	109,424	275,200	.40
Wyoming	8,933	22,800	.39
50 states and Washington, D.C.	4,735,730	13,809,000	.34

SOURCE: U.S. Office of Education unpublished data on residence and migration of college students, fall 1968. Estimates derived by the Carnegie Commission staff using Bureau of the Census *Current Population Reports,* Ser. P-25, nos. 375 and 416, and 1960 census data for the states.

Appendix E:
Ratio of Residents Enrolled as First-Time Undergraduates in Institutions in State to Number of High School Graduates (Fall 1968)

State	Students remaining	High school graduates	Ratio
Alabama	18,980	45,799	.41
Alaska	670	2,905	.23
Arizona	18,853	21,054	.90
Arkansas	11,845	25,274	.47
California	182,822	256,235	.71
Colorado	15,728	29,989	.52
Connecticut	15,239	38,974	.39
Delaware	2,180	7,121	.31
District of Columbia	3,287	6,822	.48
Florida	36,724	67,214	.55
Georgia	18,567	55,470	.33
Hawaii	5,280	11,230	.47
Idaho	5,878	11,751	.50
Illinois	75,549	139,253	.54
Indiana	27,816	70,033	.40
Iowa	19,138	45,871	.42
Kansas	19,284	33,693	.57
Kentucky	17,337	40,326	.43
Louisiana	21,862	47,897	.46

State	Students remaining	High school graduates	Ratio
Maine	3,586	15,014	.24
Maryland	18,383	48,937	.38
Massachusetts	40,037	76,530	.52
Michigan	59,935	126,558	.47
Minnesota	28,319	61,686	.46
Mississippi	17,367	29,225	.59
Missouri	28,955	59,851	.48
Montana	5,568	11,642	.48
Nebraska	11,076	22,871	.48
Nevada	1,946	5,053	.39
New Hampshire	2,855	10,086	.28
New Jersey	27,775	95,082	.29
New Mexico	6,135	15,676	.39
New York	126,386	223,000	.57
North Carolina	23,698	64,994	.36
North Dakota	5,771	10,768	.54
Ohio	63,296	147,530	.43
Oklahoma	20,200	35,445	.57
Oregon	17,371	31,022	.56
Pennsylvania	56,884	171,275	.33
Rhode Island	5,513	11,189	.49
South Carolina	10,539	34,367	.31
South Dakota	5,960	12,497	.48
Tennessee	19,551	48,522	.40
Texas	76,484	133,192	.57
Utah	9,128	16,999	.54
Vermont	1,767	7,968	.22
Virginia	19,196	57,790	.33
Washington	33,156	49,190	.67
West Virginia	9,947	26,899	.37
Wisconsin	30,555	71,473	.43
Wyoming	2,922	5,293	.55
50 states and Washington, D.C.	1,307,300	2,701,000	.48

SOURCE: U.S. Office of Education unpublished data on residence and migration of college students, fall 1968. U.S. Office of Education, *1969 Digest of Educational Statitistics,* Washington, D.C., 1969.

Appendix F: Ratio of Residents Enrolled as First-Time Undergraduates in Institutions in Any State to High School Graduates (1968)

State	Student residents	Number of high school graduates	Ratio
Alabama	21,475	45,799	.47
Alaska	1,334	2,905	.46
Arizona	20,548	21,054	.98
Arkansas	13,762	25,274	.54
California	192,129	256,235	.75
Colorado	18,357	29,989	.61
Connecticut	26,190	38,974	.67
Delaware	3,453	7,121	.48
District of Columbia	5,526	6,822	.81
Florida	43,804	67,214	.65
Georgia	22,471	55,470	.41
Hawaii	7,196	11,230	.64
Idaho	7,264	11,751	.62
Illinois	94,191	139,253	.68
Indiana	32,531	70,033	.46
Iowa	24,123	45,871	.53
Kansas	21,522	33,693	.64
Kentucky	19,948	40,326	.49
Louisiana	23,663	47,897	.49

State	Student residents	Number of high school graduates	Ratio
Maine	5,157	15,014	.34
Maryland	25,468	48,937	.52
Massachusetts	50,380	76,530	.66
Michigan	64,349	126,558	.51
Minnesota	32,352	61,686	.52
Mississippi	18,668	29,225	.64
Missouri	33,782	59,851	.56
Montana	6,763	11,642	.58
Nebraska	12,777	22,871	.56
Nevada	2,717	5,053	.54
New Hampshire	4,527	10,086	.45
New Jersey	56,027	95,082	.59
New Mexico	7,766	15,676	.50
New York	157,537	223,000	.71
North Carolina	26,427	64,994	.41
North Dakota	6,725	10,768	.62
Ohio	74,892	147,530	.51
Oklahoma	22,098	35,445	.62
Oregon	19,709	31,022	.64
Pennsylvania	74,198	171,275	.43
Rhode Island	7,471	11,189	.67
South Carolina	13,252	34,367	.39
South Dakota	6,935	12,497	.55
Tennessee	22,469	48,522	.46
Texas	81,033	133,192	.61
Utah	9,668	16,999	.57
Vermont	2,734	7,968	.34
Virginia	27,280	57,790	.47
Washington	35,828	49,190	.73
West Virginia	11,283	26,899	.42
Wisconsin	34,043	71,473	.48
Wyoming	3,684	5,293	.70
50 states and Washington, D.C.	1,557,486	2,701,000	.58

SOURCES: U.S. Office of Education unpublished data on residence and migration of college students, fall 1968. U.S. Office of Education, *1969 Digest of Educational Statistics,* Washington, D.C., 1969.

Appendix G: Percent Change in Ratio from 1963 to 1968

$Ratio = \dfrac{\text{First-time student residents}}{\text{High school graduates}}$				$Ratio = \dfrac{\text{First-time students remaining}}{\text{High school graduates}}$			
State	1963 ratio	1968 ratio	Percent change	State	1963 ratio	1968 ratio	Percent change
Alabama	.3229	.4688	45.1	Alabama	.2529	.4144	63.8
Alaska	.4681	.4592	−1.9	Alaska	.2058	.2306	12.0
Arizona	.6108	.9759	59.7	Arizona	.5293	.8954	69.1
Arkansas	.4732	.5445	15.0	Arkansas	.4041	.4686	15.9
California	.8067	.7498	−7.0	California	.7664	.7134	−6.9
Colorado	.5532	.6121	10.6	Colorado	.4456	.5244	17.6
Connecticut	.5744	.6719	16.9	Connecticut	.3158	.3910	23.8
Delaware	.4535	.4849	6.9	Delaware	.2357	.3061	29.8
District of Columbia	.6348	.8100	27.5	District of Columbia	.3258	.4818	47.8
Florida	.6126	.6517	6.3	Florida	.4925	.5463	10.9
Georgia	.3557	.4051	13.8	Georgia	.2815	.3347	18.8
Hawaii	.4928	.6407	30.0	Hawaii	.3265	.4701	43.9
Idaho	.6225	.6181	−0.7	Idaho	.4725	.5002	5.8
Illinois	.6277	.6764	7.7	Illinois	.4860	.5425	11.6
Indiana	.4424	.4645	4.9	Indiana	.3694	.3971	7.4
Iowa	.4812	.5258	9.2	Iowa	.3673	.4172	13.5
Kansas	.5406	.6387	18.1	Kansas	.4640	.5723	23.3
Kentucky	.4684	.4946	5.5	Kentucky	.3942	.4299	9.0
Louisiana	.4650	.4940	6.2	Louisiana	.4248	.4564	7.4

Ratio = First-time student residents / High school graduates				Ratio = First-time students remaining / High school graduates			
State	*1963 ratio*	*1968 ratio*	*Percent change*	*State*	*1963 ratio*	*1968 ratio*	*Percent change*
Maine	.3187	.3434	7.7	Maine	.2118	.2388	12.7
Maryland	.5138	.5204	1.2	Maryland	.3702	.3756	1.4
Massachusetts	.5372	.6583	22.5	Massachusetts	.4125	.5231	26.8
Michigan	.4509	.5084	12.7	Michigan	.4041	.4735	17.1
Minnesota	.4570	.5244	14.7	Minnesota	.3896	.4590	17.8
Mississippi	.5228	.6387	22.1	Mississippi	.4786	.5942	24.1
Missouri	.4928	.5644	14.5	Missouri	.4045	.4837	19.5
Montana	.5904	.5809	−1.6	Montana	.4742	.4782	0.8
Nebraska	.5407	.5586	3.3	Nebraska	.4585	.4842	5.6
Nevada	.6950	.5377	−22.6	Nevada	.4843	.3851	−20.4
New Hampshire	.3716	.4488	20.7	New Hampshire	.2077	.2830	36.2
New Jersey	.5291	.5892	11.3	New Jersey	.2679	.2921	9.0
New Mexico	.4828	.4954	2.6	New Mexico	.3486	.3913	12.2
New York	.4666	.7064	51.3	New York	.3332	.5667	70.0
North Carolina	.3617	.4066	12.4	North Carolina	.3219	.3646	13.2
North Dakota	.5056	.6245	23.5	North Dakota	.4185	.5359	28.0
Ohio	.4507	.5076	12.6	Ohio	.3686	.4290	16.3
Oklahoma	.5378	.6234	15.9	Oklahoma	.4771	.5698	19.4
Oregon	.5446	.6353	16.6	Oregon	.4561	.5599	22.7
Pennsylvania	.3816	.4332	13.5	Pennsylvania	.2843	.3321	16.8
Rhode Island	.4483	.6677	48.9	Rhode Island	.3008	.4927	63.7
South Carolina	.3439	.3856	12.1	South Carolina	.2687	.3066	14.1
South Dakota	.5110	.5549	8.5	South Dakota	.4237	.4769	12.5
Tennessee	.4195	.4630	10.3	Tennessee	.3331	.4029	20.9
Texas	.5689	.6083	6.9	Texas	.5264	.5742	9.0
Utah	.5603	.5687	1.4	Utah	.5291	.5369	1.4
Vermont	.3524	.3431	−2.6	Vermont	.2233	.2217	−0.7
Virginia	.4667	.4720	1.1	Virginia	.3110	.3321	6.7
Washington	.5735	.7283	26.9	Washington	.5059	.6740	33.2
West Virginia	.3762	.4194	11.4	West Virginia	.3209	.3697	15.2
Wisconsin	.4128	.4763	15.3	Wisconsin	.3519	.4275	21.4
Wyoming	.6311	.6960	10.2	Wyoming	.4547	.5520	21.3
United States	.5124	.5766	12.5	United States	.4171	.4840	16.0

Appendix H: State Per Capita Appropriations for Higher Education

State	Appropriation per capita	Rank per capita
Alabama	$22.18	47
Alaska	57.70	2
Arizona	47.57	5
Arkansas	29.12	40
California	41.49	14
Colorado	50.38	4
Connecticut	32.58	33
Delaware	37.26	19
Florida	36.18	22
Georgia	33.09	30
Hawaii	73.70	1
Idaho	45.12	7
Illinois	43.52	9
Indiana	33.83	27
Iowa	36.42	21
Kansas	36.91	20
Kentucky	31.23	36
Louisiana	34.18	25

State	Appropriation per capita	Rank per capita
Maine	28.43	41
Maryland	31.22	37
Massachusetts	20.62	49
Michigan	39.16	16
Minnesota	38.07	17
Mississippi	33.44	29
Missouri	28.38	42
Montana	42.74	10
Nebraska	32.96	32
Nevada	33.01	31
New Hampshire	15.13	50
New Jersey	21.78	48
New Mexico	41.71	12
New York	41.52	13
North Carolina	35.46	23
North Dakota	38.07	17
Ohio	24.73	46
Oklahoma	27.80	43
Oregon	46.64	6
Pennsylvania	30.25*	38*
Rhode Island	34.05	26
South Carolina	27.26	44
South Dakota	32.06	34
Tennessee	25.68	45
Texas	31.26	35
Utah	42.73	11
Vermont	33.71	28
Virginia	29.96	39
Washington	56.94	3
West Virginia	34.50	24
Wisconsin	41.27	15
Wyoming	44.65	8
TOTAL U.S.	34.98	

*Estimate

SOURCE: From *The Chronicle of Higher Education*, vol. V, no. 3, October 12, 1970, p. 1.

Appendix I:
Net "In" and "Out" Migration of Students (1968)

State	Students enrolled	Out of	Into	Net
Alabama	91,399	11,388	13,882	2,494
Alaska	3,013	2,316	620	—1,696
Arizona	76,384	7,399	14,284	6,885
Arkansas	48,365	7,625	7,377	—248
California	822,296	47,290	59,378	12,088
Colorado	92,688	11,205	28,860	17,655
Connecticut	97,681	43,281	22,156	—21,125
Delaware	13,500	6,152	5,565	—587
District of Columbia	61,315	9,740	47,142	37,402
Florida	176,973	31,845	27,711	—4,134
Georgia	102,614	16,578	22,241	5,663
Hawaii	25,015	7,899	5,275	—2,624
Idaho	24,495	7,506	5,565	—1,941
Illinois	352,767	81,039	48,585	—32,454
Indiana	172,090	21,418	47,913	26,495
Iowa	97,740	22,477	28,282	5,805
Kansas	90,360	12,647	18,963	6,316
Kentucky	90,204	12,704	21,596	8,892
Louisiana	112,529	8,962	14,013	5,051

State	Students enrolled	Out of	Into	Net
Maine	21,491	6,765	7,567	802
Maryland	105,659	35,324	19,997	−15,327
Massachusetts	240,528	42,931	80,247	37,316
Michigan	294,437	21,572	38,874	17,302
Minnesota	125,617	18,429	22,199	3,770
Mississippi	62,960	6,861	8,075	1,214
Missouri	154,428	22,011	38,831	16,820
Montana	24,376	5,059	3,777	−1,282
Nebraska	59,634	7,959	14,862	6,903
Nevada	9,355	3,373	1,675	−1,282
New Hampshire	23,007	7,617	12,268	4,651
New Jersey	149,506	117,256	18,546	−98,710
New Mexico	36,833	6,595	6,951	356
New York	686,466	137,650	81,934	−55,716
North Carolina	125,076	12,591	36,147	23,556
North Dakota	24,130	4,730	4,001	−729
Ohio	320,982	51,017	61,378	10,361
Oklahoma	96,437	9,036	15,524	6,488
Oregon	84,405	9,996	14,753	4,757
Pennsylvania	339,690	77,441	66,844	−10,597
Rhode Island	33,518	8,650	12,120	3,470
South Carolina	46,905	11,514	11,428	−86
South Dakota	26,786	4,476	6,172	1,696
Tennessee	117,264	13,159	33,196	20,037
Texas	353,801	21,892	34,910	13,018
Utah	64,962	3,125	21,036	17,911
Vermont	16,926	3,951	10,166	6,215
Virginia	100,196	39,313	24,543	−14,770
Washington	124,048	13,204	18,594	5,390
West Virginia	56,603	6,545	16,286	9,741
Wisconsin	156,239	17,386	33,997	16,611
Wyoming	12,286	3,452	2,658	−794

Appendix J:
Resolution of the Education Commission of the States, July 10, 1970

WHEREAS State boundaries create an artifical barrier to educational opportunities for many students who are border area residents and for others whose educational objectives could be met better through pursuing education in another state; and

WHEREAS Some states do not have a sufficient number or distribution of diverse types of post–high school institutions to meet increasing enrollment pressures and cannot offer opportunities to enroll in a complete range of professional, technical, liberal arts programs; and

WHEREAS Most states have responded to pressures to offset educational costs by very significant increases in non-resident tuition charges, thus restricting student mobility between the states;

NOW, THEREFORE, BE IT RESOLVED that the Education Commission of the States investigate the feasibility of a national system to facilitate the exchange of students among the various states through an arrangement whereby a state and/or national balance sheet of imported to exported students is maintained.

Appendix K:
Iowa Tuition Grants Program

In 1969, the state of Iowa introduced a tuition grant program for students attending private colleges. In a recent article describing it, the Iowa program was characterized as that state's first transfusion of state tax money into the financially pressed private colleges. The program was introduced at a time when total enrollment at Iowa private colleges had dropped for two successive years.

Under the Iowa program, the tuition grant is available to financially needy full-time students attending accredited private institutions. Assuming full financial need, the maximum amount of the tuition grant is equal to the total tuition and fees at the private institution attended by the student less the average amount of tuition at state universities (established at $610 for the first year of the program), but in no event more than $1,000.

Financial need of the applicants for grants is determined by the Educational Testing Service based upon statements provided by the students and their families.

For the first year of the program $1.5 million was available for tuition grants. Average grants of $750 were awarded to 1,982 students at 31 private colleges and universities in Iowa.

Dr. Roy Wellborne, executive director of the State Higher Education Facilities Commission, which has the responsibility of administering this program, said that it would have taken $4.1 million to provide the maximum grant allowed to each applicant who could demonstrate financial need. This level of funding would have made it possible to give grants to the additional 4,693 students who qualified under the guidelines for some aid, but who did not receive it because they were judged less needy than the almost 2,000 grant recipients.

It is anticipated that $3 million will be available for these grants in 1970–71.

Appendix L:
Selected Proposals for General Support Grants to Colleges and Universities

Howard Bowen[1]

1   The Federal Government would calculate for a series of past years the national average cost of instruction per student (f.t.e.) for various classes of students stratified by course of study (i.e., liberal arts, engineering, law, etc.) and by class level (i.e., Freshman-sophomore, junior-senior, graduate, etc.).

2   By analysis of these figures and of the plans of a sample of institutions, an estimate of the cost in each category for the coming year would be made.

3   Each institution would estimate the number of students (f.t.e.) it expects in each category in the coming year.

4   A provisional cost-of-education grant to each institution for each student category would be calculated as some fraction (say one-half) of the estimated increase in cost multiplied by the number of students.

5   A provisional enrollment grant to each institution for each student category would be calculated as a fraction (say one-half) of estimated total cost per student in the preceding year multiplied by the increase in the number of students (f.t.e.).

6   The provisional cost-of-education and enrollment grants would be paid to the institution in installments during the year.

7   When the year had been completed and the actual costs and enrollments were known, the final grant would be determined. Any excess or deficiency

[1] SOURCE: Howard R. Bowen, *The Finance of Higher Education,* Carnegie Commission on Higher Education, 1968, pp. 18–19.

in payment compared with the provisional grant would be adjusted as a reduction or addition to the next year's provisional grant. The system would resemble a pay-as-you-go income tax.

8   The grant for the first year of the plan would be continued into the second and subsequent years of the program, and further additions would be made according to the formula each year. The Federal government, then, would gradually assume an increasing role in the finance of educational costs.

Quie Institutional Grants Bill[2]

Section 4 (2)   The amount of the grant to which an institution (four-year institution) is entitled under this subsection for a fiscal year shall be based on the number of baccalaureate degrees awarded by such institution during the preceding fiscal year and shall be determined in accordance with the following table:

If the number of baccalaureate degrees awarded was:	The amount of the grant is:
Not over 200	$500 for each degree
Over 200 but not over 500	$100,000 plus $400 for each degree in excess of 200
Over 500 but not over 1,000	$220,000 plus $300 for each degree in excess of 500
Over 1,000 but not over 2,000	$370,000 plus $200 for each degree in excess of 1,000
Over 2,000	$570,000 plus $100 for each degree in excess of 2,000

(b)   If the sums appropriated for any fiscal year for making grants under this section are not sufficient to pay in full the total amounts that all institutions of higher education are entitled to receive under subsection (a), the grant to each such institution shall be an amount which bears the same ratio to the amount to which it is entitled under subsection (a) as such sums appropriated bear to the total amounts all institutions are entitled to receive under subsection (a).

[2] SOURCE: H.R. 16622, pp. 3 and 4, introduced by Mr. Quie in the 2nd session of the 91st Congress, March 24, 1970.

Illinois proposal for grants to private institutions[3]

The Commission recommends a program of annual direct grants from public funds to the private institutions in Illinois for the support of their current educational and general operations. These grants are designed to assist the State and the institutions to achieve the objectives which have just been outlined.

The Commission has considered many possible methods for determining the amount and allocation of these grants, and has concluded that the simplest, most equitable, and most appropriate system for this State will be an annual allocation to each eligible private institution of

$500 for each Illinois State Scholarship and Grant recipient enrolled, including recipients of honorary scholarships; plus

$100 for all other full-time equivalent undergraduate students enrolled in the freshman and sophomore years; and

$200 for all other full-time equivalent undergraduate students enrolled in the junior and senior years.

Cost-of-education supplement[4]

Both the task force of the Department of Health, Education, and Welfare and the Carnegie Commission on Higher Education have proposed granting funds to institutions through cost-of-education supplements.

The Commission proposal is:

To encourage colleges to participate more fully in the move toward equality of educational opportunity and to aid them in meeting increased educational costs including those related to this effort, the Commission recommends that the federal government grant cost-of-education supplements to colleges and universities based on the numbers and levels of students holding federal grants enrolled in the institutions.

Amounts of Grants. Accredited colleges and universities, and institutions deemed potentially eligible for accreditation except for their recent date of establishment, would receive the following amounts for each federal grant holder enrolled:

[3] SOURCE: *Strengthening Private Higher Education in Illinois,* March 1969, pp. 46–47.

[4] SOURCE: Carnegie Commission on Higher Education, June 1970 supplement to the 1968 Special Report *Quality and Equality: Revised Recommendations — New Levels of Federal Responsibility for Higher Education,* p. 21.

	1970–71	1979–80
Undergraduate	$ 500	$1,000
First-level graduate	1,000	1,500
Doctoral	3,500	5,000

HEW proposes:[5]

The cost-of-education allowance would be $100 per student aided plus 25 percent of each individual grant in excess of $200. Thus, an institution's allotment for each term would be based upon the total amount of federal grants received by its students during that term. No proprietary institution would be eligible for a cost-of-education allowance.

Further, a cost-of-education allowance should be applied to funds distributed under the NDEA loan program and the college work-study program to help offset the cost of educating federally induced enrollments. It is recommended that each institution receive a sum equal to 25 percent of the amount of federal funds it receives under these programs.

HEW also recommended increasing the cost-of-education supplement for doctoral fellowship holders to $5,000.

Voucher proposals[6]

Some proposals channel all public money to students in financial need and aid institutions by permitting them to charge closer to full cost tuition. The recent Wisconsin proposal is an example of this type:

Recommendation: Adopt a voucher system for higher education whereby any qualified Wisconsin high school graduate may attend any accredited non-profit post-secondary school, college, or university in Wisconsin, public or private, subject to the enrollment limits and other requirements of the school. All students will receive a basic grant of $500 and a supplementary grant based on their financial ability to pay. Institutions will collect full tuition from the students, rather than receive appropriations from the legislature. This program will be called the Higher Education Opportunity Program.

[5] SOURCE: HEW report, *Toward a Long-Range Plan for Federal Financial Support for Higher Education,* January 1969, p. 31.

[6] SOURCE: Final report of the Governor's Commission on Education, *A Forward Look,* Department of Administration, state of Wisconsin, November 1970, p. 43.

Carnegie Commission on Higher Education
Publications in Print

THE CAPITOL AND THE CAMPUS:
STATE RESPONSIBILITY FOR POSTSECONDARY
EDUCATION
*a report and recommendations by the
Commission*

THE NEW DEPRESSION IN HIGHER
EDUCATION:
A STUDY OF FINANCIAL CONDITIONS AT 41
COLLEGES AND UNIVERSITIES
Earl F. Cheit

FROM ISOLATION TO MAINSTREAM:
PROBLEMS OF THE COLLEGES FOUNDED
FOR NEGROES
*a report and recommendations by the
Commission*

FINANCING MEDICAL EDUCATION:
AN ANALYSIS OF ALTERNATIVE POLICIES
AND MECHANISMS
Rashi Fein and Gerald I. Weber

HIGHER EDUCATION IN NINE COUNTRIES:
A COMPARATIVE STUDY OF COLLEGES AND
UNIVERSITIES ABROAD
*Barbara B. Burn, Philip G. Altbach, Clark Kerr,
and James A. Perkins*

LESS TIME, MORE OPTIONS:
EDUCATION BEYOND THE HIGH SCHOOL
*a special report and recommendations
by the Commission*

BRIDGES TO UNDERSTANDING:
INTERNATIONAL PROGRAMS OF AMERICAN
COLLEGES AND UNIVERSITIES
Irwin T. Sanders and Jennifer C. Ward

HIGHER EDUCATION AND THE NATION'S
HEALTH:
POLICIES FOR MEDICAL AND DENTAL
EDUCATION
*a special report and recommendations by the
Commission*

GRADUATE AND PROFESSIONAL EDUCATION,
1980:
A SURVEY OF INSTITUTIONAL PLANS
Lewis B. Mayhew

THE AMERICAN COLLEGE AND AMERICAN
CULTURE:
SOCIALIZATION AS A FUNCTION OF HIGHER
EDUCATION
Oscar and Mary F. Handlin

RECENT ALUMNI AND HIGHER EDUCATION:
A SURVEY OF COLLEGE GRADUATES
Joe L. Spaeth and Andrew M. Greeley

CHANGE IN EDUCATIONAL POLICY:
SELF-STUDIES IN SELECTED COLLEGES AND
UNIVERSITIES
Dwight R. Ladd

THE OPEN-DOOR COLLEGES:
POLICIES FOR COMMUNITY COLLEGES
*a special report and recommendations by the
Commission*

QUALITY AND EQUALITY: REVISED
RECOMMENDATIONS
NEW LEVELS OF FEDERAL RESPONSIBILITY
FOR HIGHER EDUCATION
*a supplement to the 1968 special report by
the Commission*

STATE OFFICIALS AND HIGHER EDUCATION:
A SURVEY OF THE OPINIONS AND
EXPECTATIONS OF POLICY MAKERS IN NINE
STATES
Heinz Eulau and Harold Quinley

A CHANCE TO LEARN:
AN ACTION AGENDA FOR EQUAL
OPPORTUNITY IN HIGHER EDUCATION
*a special report and recommendations by the
Commission*

ACADEMIC DEGREE STRUCTURES:
INNOVATIVE APPROACHES
PRINCIPLES OF REFORM IN DEGREE
STRUCTURES IN THE UNITED STATES
Stephen H. Spurr

COLLEGES OF THE FORGOTTEN AMERICANS:
A PROFILE OF STATE COLLEGES AND
REGIONAL UNIVERSITIES
E. Alden Dunham

FROM BACKWATER TO MAINSTREAM:
A PROFILE OF CATHOLIC HIGHER
EDUCATION
Andrew M. Greeley

ALTERNATIVE METHODS OF FEDERAL
FUNDING FOR HIGHER EDUCATION
Ron Wolk

INVENTORY OF CURRENT RESEARCH ON
HIGHER EDUCATION 1968
Dale M. Heckman and Warren Bryan Martin

QUALITY AND EQUALITY:
NEW LEVELS OF FEDERAL RESPONSIBILITY
FOR HIGHER EDUCATION
*a special report and recommendations by the
Commission, with 1970 revisions*

*The following reprints are available from the Carnegie Commission on
Higher Education, 1947 Center Street, Berkeley, California 94704*

. . . AND WHAT PROFESSORS THINK
*Seymour Martin Lipset and
Everett Carll Ladd, Jr.*

DEMAND AND SUPPLY
IN U.S. HIGHER EDUCATION:
A PROGRESS REPORT
Roy Radner and Leonard S. Miller

THE UNHOLY ALLIANCE
AGAINST THE CAMPUS
Kenneth Keniston and Michael Lerner

PRECARIOUS PROFESSORS:
NEW PATTERNS OF REPRESENTATION
Joseph W. Garbarino